Rhythmic African Spirituality
in Sports, Dance, Music and Art

by
William F. Gunn, Jr.

Published by
The Kemetic Institute for Leadership and Human Development

Permission to use the late Listervelt Middleton's Poems granted by Ernestine Middleton

Library of Congress Control Number: 2006907133
ISBN: 0-9788021-0-1

The cover is a painting by Tyrone Geter
Cover design by Tyrone Geter

Rhythmic African Spirituality in Sports, Dance, Music and Art

by
William F. Gunn, Jr. Ed.D

Kemetic Institute for Leadership and Human Development

2006

Dedication

This book is dedicated to all the students that I have taught at Benedict College over the last forty-two years. All of you have brought me more joy than you could ever imagine. I would also like to dedicate the book to my dear friend Dr. Listervelt Middleton who, through his poetry, helped us to understand the true origin of things and left our children with a charge which we must help them honor; and above all, I dedicate this book to my two sons, Rodney and Eldridge, and my wife, Charlie Mae, who have always provided a happy home environment for me to work.

On The Origins Of Things

look around you Black child
your creation is everywhere
though painted, distorted,
given new names
they bear your prints
just the same
so sharpen your eyes
tune your ear
so you'll know what you see
understand what you hear

you were first to write
the first to read
humanity sprang
from your black seed
for 110,000 years
you were here alone
and then the Caucasian man
was born
behind the ice
inside the cold
a chill set in
this new man's soul
other minds have been credited
with the things
they learned from you:
Newton, Pythagoras, Kepler
and Galileo too

sharpen your ear
so you'll know what you see
understand what you hear

you made the serpent the symbol
of the healing arts
and African justice
was goddess Maat
who weighted herself
against the African soul
truth and justice blind-fold
the George Washington Monument
is yours too
a copy of the Egyptian
tekenu
the symbol of the Black world's
powers of creation
the Black man's penis
in devine procreation
the king of Southern Egypt
wore the white crown
keep listening
and you'll catch your mouth
when you learn that
the central government in Egypt
was known as the White House
sharpen your eyes
tune your ear
so you'll know what you see
understand what you hear

your God Osiris
was restored to life
long before Buddha
long before Chirst
and today
what you call the Madonna and Child
is but the first Black family
worshiped 'long the Nile
and when you feel the Spirit -
the Holy Ghost
you should know
it started at Abydos
where God Osiris body was laid
the Holy land
where Africans prayed
minute by minute
hour by hour
as you lose your history
you lose your power
so sharpen your eyes
tune your ear
so you'll know what you see
understand what you hear

~ Dr. Listervelt Middleton

Rhythmic African Spirituality

in

Sports, Dance, Music and Art

by William F. Gunn, Jr.

Contents

Acknowledgments

I am indebted to many persons who helped me complete this project. I would like to thank Julian Shabazz for guiding me through each step of the publishing process. The suggestions about style and content that were made by Ms. Davida McDonald and Ms. Vivian Counts were invaluable. I would like to give special thanks to Dr. Gwenda Greene and Ms. Ruby Blair for editing the book and Mr. Tyrone Geter for allowing me to use one of his paintings on the book cover.

I also extend thanks to my early study group members in the Association for the Study of Classical African Civilizations, particularly Dr. Burnett Gallman, Mr. Jerome Boykin, Mr. Joe Benton, Minister Derrick Jackson and Seitu Amenwasu; and to Alvin Cannon for being so persistent in bringing African-centered scholars to Columbia, South Carolina. The many group sessions and lectures by African- centered scholars helped me to clarify many spiritual, social, psychological, and historical issues that apply to African People.

I am eternally grateful to the African-centered scholars who shaped my understanding of African people. I am sure that if I had not read the books and articles by such scholars as Dr. Richard King, Dr. Ivan Van Sertima, Dr. Cheikh Anta Diop, Mr. Anthony Browder, Dr. John Henrik Clarke, Dr. Yosef ben Jochannon, Dr. Wade Nobles, Dr. Amos Wilson, Dr. Barbara Sizemore, Dr. Marimba Ani, and Mr. James Smalls, I would still be psychologically enslaved, believing that Europeans were the first to bring civilization to the world.

Foreword

Even though I am a chemist and educator by western training, it is my African spirituality that helps me to embrace the interrelatedness of all human interaction with and response to the "seen" and "unseen" forces (rhythm) of cosmic energies. Dance, particularly dance of the African diaspora, is a physical, dynamic manifestation of being in complete rhythmic balance and harmony with the universal creator and creation. This manifestation requires the total release of "personal will to divine will" (Carolyn Myss, The Anatomy of the Spirit), a feat easily accomplished by children who move intuitively and spontaneously in perfect rhythm in response to certain sounds and tempos.

The author shares with us his ingenious evolutionary journey of revealing not only the spiritual essence of dance, but also the intrinsic application of the natural sciences (chemistry, physics, biology, etc) through which dance is manifested. Additionally, the author dispels Eurocentric attitudes that dance is a frivolous indulgence or arbitrary response to with no connection to intelligence, health and heightened levels of spiritual enlightenment. He explains that the music and movement patterns of the current hip-hop culture are both good and bad. Sometimes they express beautiful rhythmic lyrics and movements and at other times produce sounds that perpetuate movements which negate the harmonious energies of the universe, resulting in a spiritual "disconnection" from the creator. Therefore, this book is equally important for our younger generation.

This book offers African Americans the opportunity to understand that our natural response to rhythmic vibrational energies should be celebrated and embraced. Movement and art are as life-essential to African Americans as the air we breathe. So as the author suggests, we must move, sing, and develop art that is in sync with the universal rhythms of the creator. Our very survival depends upon it.

Vivian Counts
Instructor of Chemistry at Benedict College

Introduction

This book consists of a series of essays that I have written over a period of about fifteen years. I started wondering why African American people made such delightful sounds, moved their bodies in such a graceful manner in dance and athletics and developed exquisite art forms. In church, I was sometimes in awe of the captivating music and the interesting movement that would develop during church service. I was always curious about what was actually stimulating the intense emotional outbursts that I often witnessed in church. When I attended the funeral of my wife's mother, I was intrigued by the testimonial Holiness-Pentecostal Service. The trance-like spiritual reality in the music, shouting and dancing, left me filled with intense feelings of a spiritual source that was physically internal and external all at the same time. I left this experience thinking that there was something extremely spiritual in the powerful shouting and dancing in the Holiness-Pentecostal Church that came from a higher source than I had previously imagined.

As a physical education teacher who taught Kinesiology, I never considered spirituality and movement in the same arena until I started trying to answer the question, why Africans seem to move in such magnificent ways and create superb movement patterns in dancing and athletics. I often ask college students if they could envision what NBA basketball was like during the segregation of white and black Americans where most of the time the teams were totally white. To make my point, I tried to paint a mental picture for them to see. I explained how slow the play was and emphasized that they played what I would call pattern basketball. In pattern basketball the team would run a specific play. The play slowly developed before there was a shot at the basket. High scoring games were seldom seen. Some players shot the ball from their chest and others shot free-throws from below the wrist. Even more ironic is that many NBA players were unable to dribble the basketball with both hands. African Americans changed the game and turned it into what to me is a true spiritual art form.

African American basketball players such as Oscar Robertson, Earl Monroe, Julius Erving, and Magic Johnson, just to mention a few of my favorites, took basketball skill level to new heights. Magic Johnson and Earl Monroe dazzled audiences with their fancy no look passes, while Oscar Robertson and Julius Erving always put on a shooting clinic. African American players like Julius Erving caused many kinesiologists to go back to the drawing board. Julius Erving seemed to defy many physical scientific laws. One such law suggests that a person cannot change direction in midair. He must establish angular momentum before leaving his base of support. Julius Erving seemed to just hang in the air and change directions at will. Today many African American athletes have revolutionized sports. They play the game with more speed, higher vertical jumps, and more agility. They have the uncanny ability to be aware of their bodies in space. The superior performances of these African American athletes led me to ask myself the question about the role of the pineal and melanin.

In the essays included in this book, I quote both Richard King and Carol Barnes frequently. They support the idea that the pineal gland is the gland that allows human beings to develop a higher conscious level, and the melanin chemical enables one to develop phenomenal physical and mental abilities. King further suggests that individuals may have a spiritual experience where they actually are in rhythmic harmony and balance with the creative forces of the cosmic universe.

The essays included are in chronological order. The first one was written in 1993 with the intent of showing a link between African spirituality and the awesome movement patterns that African people are able to perfect. The second was written in 1998 and was inspired by my contact with many African Americans who knew little about their own history and culture, but cherished European history and culture. This unfortunate state motivated me to try and explain how beautiful African people are in dance, music and the production of art works, and that our culture has a soulful foundation that was conceived on the notion that being in harmony and balance with the creative forces of nature was important. I further emphasized the fact that if one is able to be in spiritual rhythm with the Devine mind of the creator, it is possible to accomplish anything.

The third essay, written in 1999, was sparked by a paper that was presented at a National Association of African American Studies Conference about the life of Tupac Shakur. Before the conference I had paid little or no attention to the music and poetry of Tupac. However, after I returned home from the conference, I began to inquire about him with my students at Benedict College. The good feeling and the admiration they had for him surprised me to no end. They encouraged me to listen to his music to better understand him as a person. I was astonished at the dichotomy in his lyrics. Sometimes they were very thuggish and violent, and at other times very empathetic and caring about the problems that young African Americans faced daily trying to survive in the community.

In listening to his music, I understood why students loved and respected Tupac. He was not only a rapper but an eloquent poet. His poem entitled "In case of my Demise" led me to compare him with Dr. Martin Luther King, Jr. in terms of their oratorical rhythmic style, the sound of their spiritual messages and the intent of their souls.

The fourth essay was written in 2001 after the marriage break up of a couple I knew very well. Each of them blamed the other for their problems. While listening to them, I felt the degree to which African Americans had lost their way trying to adjust to the European competitive way of life. Too often in the European model of marriage one partner is usually subservient to the other. This was unlike the ancient African model where each partner understood how they complemented each other and that this complementarity enhanced their ability to move to a higher consciousness and become one with the creative forces of the cosmic universe.

In an effort to make this point, emphasis was placed on how the ancient Kametes created harmony and balance between the souls of the female principle of Ma'at and the male principle of Tehuti. This provided the opportunity for the mind of Tehuti that provides knowledge and insight to merge with the heart of Ma'at who provides rhythmic harmony to the soul. In this case, the merger of the mind and heart allows the souls of the male and female to complete each other and become one.

The fifth essay, written in 2002, was the result of what has been my major interest over the years. I marvel at the movement patterns that African Americans are able to perform in sports and dance. In 2003, I continued to try and articulate the awesome movement patterns of African people by developing an essay where I compared Brazilian Capoeira with African American Hip Hop, and ultimately attempted to explain how all of these sensational body movements are a function of the Africans desire to be in harmony and balance with the universal forces of nature.

The remaining parts in this book of essays were written in 2006. One is a collection of thoughts composed after I attended a fundraiser for South African children. In this short essay, I simply express my feelings after hearing and feeling the power of the rhythm of the drumbeat. In the last essay, I share my reflections on how writing these essays was an enlightening and divine experience.

All the essays are probably written more like poetry, depending upon intuitive knowledge rather than just deductive reasoning. The ancestors appreciated and cherished their spiritual relationship with the rhythmic cosmic universe and used it as a means to discern truth. I preferred to try and use the ancestors' method in developing these essays.

Dance is movement of various degrees (slow to fast). Movements cause vibrations that in turn produce sounds. We don't hear all soundwaves (resulting from these vibrations), but we are affected by them, nevertheless. The vibrating (dancing) body produces sound ~ kinetic intermittence at regular intervals ~ just like the musical tones produced by a vibrating string of an instrument.

Dance is much more than sensation and pleasure. It is life and unity with nature. The proper rhythm of the dance elevates the dancer to a higher realm. His/her body becomes a medium which, through connecting to the ancestors, becomes the bearer of all the forces of nature. The dancer possessed by his deified ancestor, is being transformed into this spirit, and is drawn into the circle of those supernatural forces in charge of the operation of fertility, victory, and the course of the stars.

Taken from Egyptian Rhythm
by Moustafa Gadalla

African Spirituality and
Rhythmic Movement
(1993)

During the late 1960s, I taught a course in Kinesiology which analyzed human movement, primarily in athletics. While teaching this course, I started to think critically about why African Americans were excelling in sports and dance. I began to consider the beautiful and complicated movement patterns that I had observed over the years. These patterns were used by African Americans to adjust to, what I am sure to them was an impossible situation, being powerless in a foreign culture. To move their bodies to the spiritual forces inherent in their psyche, I feel, gave them a sense of power and well-being, even if only temporary.

Sports and dance gave African Americans the opportunity to engage their African spirituality and move their bodies in profoundly graceful and rhythmic fashions. They moved with uncanny kinesthetic awareness that reflected poetry in motion and were able to create movement patterns in dance that are absolutely mystifying. In many cases, they moved their bodies in a poly-rhythmic fashion with the head, arms, legs and feet moving at different rhythmic beats. For example, the head and shoulders might be moving at one rhythm and hips and feet at yet another. Even more ironic is the fact that these body parts moved in different directions. The head moved in a lateral plane, the hips in a horizontal transverse plane and the arms in a sagittal plane–while at the same time never missing the tempo of the music.

One might wonder why African American people are able to move their bodies with such enchanting beauty. More than likely it is because rhythmic movement is a part of their cultural foundation.

In the African culture, rhythmic dance movements were performed at harvest time and even at funerals and weddings. Each dance had its own meaning and expressed a spiritual, soulful experience. To view African dance movement leaves most individuals amazed at the depth of expression that is exhibited through various movement patterns and rhythms. These variations in movement patterns are astonishing. The intuitive creative movement seems as if the body and soul are in union with the ultimate spiritual forces that govern the universe.

The ancient Egyptians (or Kamites or Kamieu as they called themselves ~ meaning the Black people of the Black land) realized thousands of years ago that the activity of the celestial bodies in the cosmos provided the key to understanding rhythmic spirituality. They observed that the sun rotated around the celestial bodies in perfect rhythm and that the stars were in perfect harmony with each other. They also noticed that as the sun rotated through the solar system, it exerted a power on earth that ultimately had an effect on the destinies of nations and individuals.

This insight led them to complete calculations on and to formulate the twelve signs of the zodiac. It was ingeniously determined that the sun regressed through one entire constellation in approximately 2,160 years and circulated through the entire zodiac in about 25,920 years. Hall (1988) called this retrograde motion "the precession of the equinoxes. This means that in the course of about 25,920 years, which constitutes one Great Solar or Platonic year, each of the twelve constellations occupies a position at the vernal equinox nearly 2,160 years, then gives its place to the previous sign."

The Kamites scrutinized with omniscient perception the

rhythmic and harmonious relationship among the heavenly bodies during each vernal equinox position. They recognized that the movement of the celestial bodies represented the ever-present spiritual force of the creator. Therefore, for them to be in harmony with this spiritual force, it was necessary to keep the body moving. This, in their minds, would force the blood in their bodies to continue its circular rhythmic flow, force the nervous system to send impulses throughout the body, and drive the endocrine glands to secrete hormones that control feelings and help open the "mental conscious door."

The opening of this door would allow the pineal gland and melanin to connect one spiritually with the outside world. They also experienced a transmigration of the soul accompanied with the precognition that the past, present, and future are one.

African people understood that everything that goes around does come back around. They danced to the music of their inner soul, moving their bodies to the circular rhythm of the universal spirit of the creator.

The drumming and dance of African people created the energy vibrations that were in sync with the forces that govern the movements of the universe. Their spiritual energy forces were intensified, which allowed them to experience the joy of achieving harmony and balance with the cosmos.

Warren (1972) observed African dance and pointed out that:

"Among the exciting sights and sound of Black Africans is not only their dance but the way it is performed. Woven throughout the pattern of African life, dancing for Africans is more than the recreation as it is for Westerners. With the music, which is inseparable from it, dancing is part of the process of living itself. The response of the body to expressions of love, joy, grief, and despair—all to the accompaniment of music, songs, and drumming—is the heritage of the African. To see an African dance is to witness his cultural past and present. Africans use their bodies to reflect their emotions, their hopes and their religions. The head moves in one rhythm, the shoulders in another, the arms in still a third, the feet in still another. Their dance is text in motion, linked to music of the drums, instruments and voices."

Rhythmic dance for African people is part of life itself; it provides the opportunity to form a union with nature. Their spiritual feelings towards all that exist around and beyond them were heightened. The right brain's function of creating harmony increases their ability to form a union of the soul with external spirit forces, while their analytical left brain brings forth the balance that allow them to actually quantify and understand how they are physical and spiritually a part of all rhythmic forces of the cosmos.

The Kamites studied the physical body and determined both the biochemical and the biophysical connection between themselves and the higher forces of nature. According to King (1990), the Kamites were aware of the pineal gland and referred to it as "the all seeing Eye of Horus." The eye was depicted as the Uraeus in the form of a serpent that was located in the middle of the forehead, the anatomical site of the pineal gland. They determined that the pineal gland secreted the black hormone, melatonin, a chemical related to brain function. This chemical was from the melanin molecule they considered to be the black seed of all life and could open the door to the unconscious mind. It would allow one to connect the soul with the spiritual forces of the universe and actually have a telepathic communication with the deities themselves. Barnes (1988) cited the fact that melanin is so profound that it is able to influence the earth's electromagnetic field and enable human beings to absorb both light waves and sound vibrations. He further indicated that melanin is in the clouds, soil, and the stars. This molecule is believed to be a primary component of creation and involved in the maintenance of the human race. It also provides the intrusive pathway to communicate with the creator.

King (1990) believes that melanin furnishes the key to understanding the source of and reason for life. He argues that human beings come from one black seed and share a collective consciousness. Through the stimulation of the pineal gland, a person is able to consciously rise above pseudo-religious beliefs and understand more clearly what caring, love, creativity and joy really mean. One is better able to perceive reality over and beyond the material and the physical, and develop a greater sense of a more spiritual world. According to King (1990), the brain, by way of the unconscious, provides the hidden doorway to "advanced laws and rhythms that span the universe feeding upon every dimension of time and space."

The ancient Africans believed thoroughly in their relationship with the universe. For them, the acquisition of knowledge was a spiritual experience. Perhaps James (1988) tells the story best, particularly in his discussion of the Egyptian Mystery System. He points out that the Kamites developed a strong ethical and moral system that was based on a serious understanding of how the universe functioned and their relationship with all that existed. As a result, they moved to the cosmic rhythms. They listened to sounds outside the body and sounds inside the body, while absorbing these sounds' energy forces. They observed all the different beautiful colors that nature could produce through the coming together of the sun, water, air, and soil; they also knew that the spirit was a mighty moving force able to maintain both balance and harmony and regenerate itself. Knowing this they not only moved to the cosmic rhythms but created new rhythms in accord with all the celestial forces that included the rotation of the earth in "sync" with the sun, stars and planets. This allowed them to be in tune with the Locus Ceruleus, that place in the brain that King (1990) interpreted from the ancient African to be the center of all previous knowledge known by our ancestors that transcends the body and opens the collective consciousness that connects one to the cosmic forces of the universe. This connection created such an intense mental, physical, and spiritual awareness that beautiful rhythmic movement was a pure expression of totality of what it meant to be alive.

African people have maintained their strong rhythmic and spiritual relationship with the creator of the universe throughout many invasions by outsiders into their homeland. They even maintained it to varying degrees through colonialism and the transatlantic slave trade. It is conceivable that the Africans' closeness to the creator of the universe is what enabled them to survive these many onslaughts from people that Bradley (1992) called the Neanderthal iceman population. This Neanderthal type, that King (1990) described as having a calcified pineal gland, committed the greatest Holocaust the world has ever known. This group was responsible for 10-15 million American Indians and Africans perishing during the slave trade. But through it all, the African adapted and maintained, to some degree, the ability to move with the spiritual forces of the creator. While working in the fields as slaves, Africans moved their bodies to songs that they intuitively and spontaneously created. Those songs described their conditions, their immediate feelings of distress, and their faith in the creator. According to Stuckey (1987), the songs, rhythms and dance unified African slaves who were from different tribes. They created the "Ring shouts" while dancing in a circle which illustrated their cultural connection to the realization of the oneness of the past, present, and future.

The African American Church, since slavery, has been the place where African people expressed their fears, hopes, frustrations, anger and love. It offered a most powerful forum for African people to move to the spiritual forces to which they were accustomed. The preaching and singing created a spiritual energy force that was so great, the rhythmic body movement was a natural consequence in order to be in harmony with the creator, if for only a brief moment in time.

The African American Church was, no doubt, the spiritual and cultural focal point in the African American community, and was partially, if not totally, responsible for the survival of African people in America. However, the church seems to no longer provide the avenue whereby African people are able to move with absolute harmony and balance in the spiritual rhythmic circle as a total way of life. In too many cases, the church projects the white Neanderthal as the person who personifies God and demands that African people be beholding to him. In this case, the African American Church becomes Anti-African and perpetuates the iceman's greedy, competitive and chauvinistic psyche.

African people all over the world must continue to struggle for psychological independence from this Neanderthal's mental trap. An example of this need is clearly shown while observing African American athletes. They move their bodies in profoundly superior fashions, yet are mentally unable to think and feel beyond the "I" or "Me" syndrome. Self is defined by how much one is able to subdue another person, rather than how self is an extension of the spiritual soul of the creator.

In similar fashion, the Hip-hop music of today is beautiful. The rhythmic style has terrific harmony; but in too many cases, the lyrics are demeaning to African American women. In the videos, women become mere sex objects, using their superior rhythmic body movements in a destructive, Neanderthal manner to sell records and videos for profit. African people must break from the trap of individual violence, sexism, and the for-profit-only mentality that is perpetuated by the Neanderthal population. African people must again move in total rhythmic harmony with the universal creator.

African people are destined to again become centered in mind, body, and soul. This will allow us to use the extraordinary power of the third eye; the all seeing "Eye of Heru" (Horus) referred to in both the Kemetic Pyramid and Coffin texts. We will be compelled to examine these texts written over three thousand years ago to intellectually discern how the Kamites theorized that the universal structure came out of the abysmal waters of Nun that gave rise to the ever moving planets, moon, stars and the life giving sun; and that goddess Ma'at typified universal harmony and balance which gave order to all values. Through universal harmony, Ma'at exemplified moral perfection that required absolute truth and justice, the supreme virtues that guided and measured all human activity.

If African people are to emerge from our deep sleep, the harmony and balance in the Ma'atian Theory must become a part of our collective consciousness. We must recognize the importance of the power of the rhythm in the cosmic universe and visualize through the pineal gland (the "The third Eye") the circular spiritual/life cycle spinning between birth, death, ancestry, and the yet-to-be-born; and understand that during this cycle, both matter and spirit move together energizing everything that moves.

African people today must continue to create beautiful rhythmic movements; but this movement must be in concert with that of the cosmic universe. In this case, unity, love and togetherness are inseparably interlaced. Just as the earth rotates with both hemispheres in unison, we must again listen to the left brain hemisphere of the Kemetic god Tehuti, who was the brilliant logical thinker, and the right brain hemisphere of the goddess Ma'at, who brought forth the feeling of love, compassion, righteousness, and justice. The rhythmic logical order of universal matter is controlled by the spirit that excites the right brain in human beings and binds us to the universal creator by way of the soul.

African people must again conceptualize the beauty of the principle of opposites and realize that as the male and female move their bodies together in rhythm with the cosmos, it is in keeping with the dynamic energy flow of the ever moving universe; and when the beautiful movements reach orgasmic perfection, the male sperm unites with the female egg, increasing the continual renewal of cosmic energy. This renewal of cosmic energy ensures the continuous harmony and balance from life to death. The spiritual cycle continues.

Life is not just today; life is forever. The energy that moves the rhythmic circle will never stop. The spiritual force of the collective oneness of everything will forever move in the rhythmic circle.

African people must always struggle to move in the cosmic circle of uniting love. Let the spiritually moving rhythmic circle never be broken.

*"The Universe is Mental-held
in the Mind of The ALL"*

*THE ALL is SPIRIT! But what is Spirit? This question
cannot be answered, for the reason that its definition is
practically that of THE ALL, which cannot be explained
or defined. Spirit is simply a name that men give to the
highest conception of Infinite Living Mind-it means "the
Real Essence"-it means Living Mind, as much superior
to Life and Mind as we know them, as the latter are
superior to mechanical Energy and Matter. Spirit
transcends our understanding, and we use the term,
merely that we may think or speak of THE ALL. For
the purposes of thought and understanding, we are
justified in thinking of Spirit as Infinite Living Mind, at
the same time acknowledging that we cannot fully
understand it. We must either do this or stop thinking
of the matter at all.*

Taken from the Kyballion written by three Initiates

Reawakening the African Mind through Dance, Music, and Art (1998)

Many African people all over the world are in a struggle to reawaken their African mind. This struggle continues in the midst of what Marimber Ani (1989) called the African Maafa, a Kiswahili word that means "disaster." Marimber used this word to describe the condition of African people. Hilliard (1997) further explained the African Maafa to mean the terroristic interruption of African civilization by European and Arab aggression. According to Hilliard, the intrusion into African civilization is multifaceted and has produced horrors like enslavement, colonization, murder, the stealing of land and property, and the systematic social, political and economic domination of Africans and African societies. The fiasco that African people find themselves in is so systematically well designed that many of the best trained African Americans with doctoral degrees have joined the Maafa against African people. These persons are often university professors who teach Western European history as if it were their own. They participate in the cultural genocide of African people.

Woodson (1933) informed African Americans about the mis-education of the Negro. During Woodson's time the mis-education was overtly bad, but after integration it became institutionally acceptable. In too many cases, African American teachers have embraced the Western European view of truth and defend it as if their lives depended upon it. If it were not for Woodson's push for a national recognition of Black History Month, African American children would hear little about their own history.

Loewen (1995), a white author, in his book entitled **Lies my Teacher Told Me** stated clearly how history has been written to glorify White Americans. Many white authors have made slavery seem like an admirable act. They suggest that since this cruel act was sanctioned by the early European Christian Church, who used the rationale that African people were less than human, that it was fine with God. The writing of textbooks by white racists and their African American companions have all but destroyed the memory that African people had of their great history.

Hilliard (1997) suggested that white America has developed what he called structures of dominance in society that control, to a large extent, what and how African Americans think. He cited education as one of the most powerful structures of dominance in determining how African American children view reality. Children in school still use books that demean African Americans. They are not exposed to African scholars like Asa Hilliard, John Henrik Clarke, Yosef A. A. Ben-Jochannan, Charles S. Finch, Wade W. Nobles, Ivan Van Sertima, Richard King, John G. Jackson, Marimber Ani and Cheikh Anta Diop just to name a few. Cheikh Anta Diop wrote a book entitled **The African Origin of Civilization Myth or Reality** that all Americans should read, particularly African American students. However, few college and university professors have exposed their students to this book or any of the authors listed above. This is probably even more true at Historically Black Colleges and Universities.

Many of the professors at Historically Black Colleges and Universities are White or of foreign birth who believe, for the most part, that all major knowledge had its origin in Europe. Unfortunately, many African American professors support this belief and operate at what Cross (1980) called the pre-encounter stage of personal development. These professors believe that the world should be guided by Western European historical and philosophical thought. They further maintain that Africa is some strange and uncivilized continent, and that integration, or assimilation, is the most effective method for solving the problems for African American people. These persons unconsciously cater to the White is beautiful and Black is ugly syndrome. Few African American professors are able to view Africa as their homeland. They persist with the idea that they are Americans forgetting that the only original Americans are the Native Americans, the so-called Indians.

The net effect of students who suffer through courses with such instructors is that many were psychologically destroyed, develop little self esteem and usually developed a negative self concept. Some, primarily middle class children, are able to develop higher self esteem. They develop the skills and knowledge that are required to function in the white world. These students ultimately began to see themselves through white eyes. They develop a white perception of reality that leads them to believe that it was the fault of those African Americans themselves who had not achieved academically. Light skin, strait hair and keen facial features are important to these students. It would be ideal if African American instructors were able to help students raise their self-esteem and develop a positive self-concept. This would help students to understand that one's cultural roots are the foundation to become centered with self. Such recognition by teachers would enable students to function as total human beings, physically, mentally, emotionally and spiritually.

African cultural philosophy is based on human beings understanding their relationship with the universal cosmos. According to Nobles (1980), this concept of reality produces a value system that is different from that of the Europeans. The European value systems emphasize individuality, uniqueness, competition, independence and survival of the fittest, while African value systems feature groupness, cooperation, collective responsibility, interdependence, and one with nature.

The Africans thoroughly believed in their relationship with the universe. For them the acquisition of knowledge was a spiritual experience. They understood that the universe represented continuous energy with one source providing its power. This source can manifest itself in any material form it so desires by way of spirits. Modern quantum physics suggests that all matter is made up of the same quantities. All objects are made of atoms that are composed of protons, neutrons and surrounded by electrons. The difference in how objects are interpreted depends upon the speed in which matter vibrates. The Africans recognized eons before Einstein developed his theory of relativity that time and matter are not constant. Time and matter are infinite and change only when they are perceived in different ways. From this simple understanding it was clear to the early African that his body was temporary, but his soul and spiritual essence was forever. The body would return to the original source that provides the chemical energy to keep the cosmos in harmony and balance. This regenerative process enables the soul and spirit to manifest themselves in a continuing everlasting circle from the past, in the present, and into future.

The Africans' realization of their profound connection with all universal forces led them to develop a strong ethical and moral system that was based on an awareness of how the universe functioned. They observed their surroundings to include the movement of the animals, all the sounds around them, and the beautiful colors that nature could produce. As a result, they moved their bodies and produced many intricate movements. These movements were in every imaginable plane and around moving axes. They were able to move with the speed and grace of a gazelle. Each movement seemed to echo the rhythmic sounds of the universe as the earth, sun and moon moved in unison with cosmic order. Movement expressed the joy of being in harmony with the creative forces and in some cases the sadness of being in disorder. However, they also danced to bring themselves back into harmony and balance.

The sounds that accompanied these movements provided the various vibrational intensities that seem to enable the African to move to a conscience level where the body's individual cell would be in rhythm with the soul of the creator. The drum would beat in sync with the heart, while the blood flowed from the heart and back again recreating every cell in the body to continue the life cycle. The sounds and movements ignited the spirits and enabled the soul of the individual to unite with the one soul of the creator. In this case the African was able to hear sounds and send an impulse through the nervous system that was interpreted in each synaptic gap in an uncommonly fast and mystical fashion.

The ancient African, in an effort to gain and maintain a relationship with the universal creative forces, strove to sensitize all of their nerve ends and activate the pineal grand. This act gave them the intuitive ability to internalize their true connection with all that existed. In ancient Memphite theology, according to Nobles (1986), the god "Ptah, emerges from the waters of **Nun** as a primeval hill and conceived in his heart everything that exists and by his utterance creates them all." Ptah proceeded through conscience will to create **Atum**, the sun God that sits upon Ptah.

Ptah completed the work of creation by willing into being four other pairs of male and female Gods: Nun and Naunet (primeval water and counter heaven); Hugh and Hauhet (the boundless and its compliment or opposite); Kuk and Kauket (darkness and its compliment or opposite); and Amun and Amaunet (the hidden and its compliment or opposite). This story of creation for the ancient African was not just a record of a series of events in time, but a speculation about the principles of life and the order of the universe.

In an attempt to understand Memphite theology, one might conclude that the ancient African understood how through conscience, will, and intent, matter came into being. Similarly, modern physics seems to be flirting with the idea that matter and conscience are of the same source. Each is energy moving at lightning speed with perhaps conscience holding matter together as an imaginary illusion. As one perceives reality in the mind, it may represent the speed at which energy is traveling. In this case, most physicists agree that all matter is made of the same material with energy vibrating at different speeds. These vibrations determine whether an object is perceived as a solid or gas. Objects vibrating with a slow intensity are perceived as a solid and those with fast vibration are perceived as gas. It would appear that through conscious mind activity, one is able to determine what objects come into existence. Radin (1997) supports the idea that the universe itself is determined by consciousness. He supports the idea that there is one mystical conscience that provides the force that binds everything in the universe together. Wolf (1996) further suggests that there is a spiritual force that encompasses the universe and a conscious soul that determines the vibrational state of all matter. He infers that this soulful conscience vibrational state determines how objects take shape in an individual's mind.

African people developed different vibrational rhythms through the drum, song and dance. Their intent was to create a vibratory state that would allow them to create the exact vibration of energy configurations to summon the presence of the ancestors. In this case, the correct vibration of their soul energy and the spiritual energy waves of the ancestors would commune. A connection would then exist between the individual's soul and the conscience universal spirit world. Sounds, body movements, and interpretations of color become one with the cosmos.

African Americans often attempt to exhibit their African roots in creating music, dance and art that illustrate their connection with the universal conscience. This is a difficult task, given the strong European indoctrination. However, the African soulful culture still exists. The old Negro Spirituals is an excellent illustration of the Africans trying to maintain a connection with their inner spiritual soul. They created songs that excited the soul and gave rise to the body's spirit. While in the fields they intuitively and spontaneously created songs that described their condition. According to Stuckey (1987), African slaves used music and danced as a means of communing with the ancestors. This was revealed in their creation of the "Ring Shouts" where they danced and sang in a circle, sometimes all night, to feel and visualize a connection with the realization of the one universal conscience.

The African slaves, like their ancient ancestors, tried hard to move and sing in such a way as to keep all aspects of the soul in harmony and balance. They were acutely aware of the soul dimensions expressed by their Kemitic predecessors. The African Kamites believed that the Ka was that part of the soul that represented the spiritual body of a person; the place that housed the other aspects of the soul, while the Ba reflected the breath of the soul; when it entered the body it activated life. The Khaba segment of the soul, according to Akbar (1994), was responsible for "sustaining sensory perceptions, the phenomena of color, harmony, rhythm, and the circulation of the blood." The Khaba to the Kamites was the sacred synthesis of the soul that produced feelings, rhythmic sounds, and body movements.

During the Ring Shouts, the African slaves conceived songs and danced in a circle, creating beautiful rhythmic sounds and body movements. They moved as if the spirits of their Kemitic brothers and sisters had engulfed their bodies and minds in order to keep them informed of the Akhu part of the soul. This part of the soul permitted a fusion between reason and attributes such as harmony, truth, justice, and compassion, and also was the seat of intelligence and mental perception which allows rhythmic harmony to gain perfection in tones and movements. Such tones were made by the African slaves by the clapping of the hands, swaying of the body and shuffling and stamping of the feet, which aroused the Kemetic Seb segment of the soul. This part of the soul was responsible for stimulating the regenerative process, the process that created harmony and balance each moment in time, and allowed human beings to reproduce their own kind. For the Kemites, the Seb was that part of the soul that provided for the magnetic attraction between man and woman in the rhythmical reproductive process that bind all human beings together.

The Kamites called the intellectual portion of the soul Putah, that phase that gave guidance to all bodily feelings. This phase of the soul was difficult for the Africans, in that to survive they were forced to adopt a new language and cultural style. However, they still created songs and dance movements that reminded them of their home land. Even though their captors, in many cases, took their most spiritual instrument, the drum, they still clapped out rhythms with their hands or shuffled and stamped rhythms with their feet. This gave them a feeling of Atum, the Kemetic most divine or eternal component of the soul that inspired perpetual continuation and integration of all other dimensions of the soul.

It was astonishing how African slaves, while laboring in the fields, were able to move their bodies to songs that they intuitively and spontaneously created. The words to the songs described their condition, while the body movements and musical tones activated the spiritual vibrations of the soul. This was apparent when one considers all of the Negro Spirituals that were sung and written during this period. Sometimes the songs expressed horror and grief and, at other times, love and joy; sometimes hope and sometimes secret codes of escape. In either case, the songs were beautifully spiritual.

Similarly to the Negro spirituals, Blues and Gospel grew out of a need to express a variety of feelings. Many Christians probably saw a conflict between the Blues and Gospel music, particularly since Blues songs dealt with relationships between men and women, love, loneliness, jealousy and infidelity. Blues told the truth about the hardships and difficulties that African people had adjusting to a foreign land where they had been accorded inhumane treatment. The Blues expressed the feelings of loneliness and being cut off from a culture that fostered togetherness and connectiveness. The Blues told the real truth about what African people were actually experiencing. This truth, in many cases, conflicted with the church's Christian doctrines. However, according to Spencer (1990), Thomas Dorsey's and Robert Wilkins' early gospel songs were little more than religious lyrics set to blues music. When they mixed Blues music and religious lyrics, church members started to move and dance to a new spiritual tone. Thus, the merger of the Blues sound and the Gospel's focus on eternal hope was born.

Gospel music, like the Blues, made church members feel good. This was a way to express, through rhythmic music, all of the difficult times that African-Americans were experiencing. Warren (1999) explained that some of the most beautiful music of all time has been born out of intense grief and suffering. Songs like "Precious Lord" and "Peace in the Valley" were composed after the tragic death of the wife and newborn son of Thomas Dorsey. While he wrote hundreds of songs in his lifetime, these were two of his masterpieces. One would suspect that this experience caused him to reach beyond the every day European reality and explore his African spiritual soul as he had never done before. On occasions the great singer Mahalia Jackson would sing these songs with such deep passion as to make the listeners feel that she had actually experienced Thomas Dorsey's pain.

Gospel music in the church was one of the major variables that aided African Americans to survive racism and economic depravation. These songs were sung with the belief that God would take care of them. They sang such songs as:

> The Lord Will Make a Way Somehow
> Stand by Me
> Sweet, Sweet Spirit
> We've Come This Far by Faith
> Take My Hand, Precious Lord
> Peace in the Valley

African Americans, like their African brothers and sisters, have always lived in a culture where songs were sung in order to experience the spirit of God. Sometimes in the Pentecostal Church the songs and rhythms brought forth such powerful energy that a person would be besieged by spirit and began

40

to dance and speak or sing in tongues. In this instance, it appears that a person would have an out of body experience and, for those moments in time, be able to commune with the spirit of God. They often would be able to speak languages previously unknown to them and move their bodies in rhythmic patterns that were in all the body planes and around all body axes. The church like no other institution helped African Americans to survive by providing the vehicle for them to feel and experience the spiritual energy of the creator.

Hip Hop music, like the Negro Spirituals, Blues, and Gospel, evolved out of a need for African Americans to express feelings about their social and economic conditions. The only difference in the emergence of Hip Hop music is that it was solely developed by inner city youth. These inner city youth were abandoned for the most part by the African American adult community. As a result, these youth not only created a new music style but a whole culture of their own. It included their own language, dress style, social organizations, and businesses. Hip Hop gave youth a forum to talk about everything and to create poetry to the beat of music. In the Hip Hop music they developed rhymes that spoke about love, drug use, being a gangster, and the hardship of having few economic resources in the inner city. Rappers like Public Enemy and Tupac Shakur developed rhymes that were explosive, provocative and in many cases dangerously clear about the problematic conditions of inner youth. Tupac raised issues about the racist society in which we live. He did it with a rage and language style that few African American adults could tolerate, but he told the truth. Young African American youth loved him because often he put beautiful poetry to rhyme. Sometimes his rhymes were not so poetic but hard and filled with anger. In either case, he spoke to the hearts of inner city youth. He felt what they felt and through his spiritual soul expressed these feelings in his music.

Lauryn Hill, comparable to the ancient Goddess Ma'at, in her recording of "The Miseducation of Lauryn Hill" developed a soaring and conceptual work that was emotionally honest. Hill seems to have reached deep within herself and, according to Good (1999), strategically blended R&B, Reggae, Hip Hop and Scripture. This recording had a spiritual tone that touched the soul of the listener and activated the right brain so that one could feel the mystical and divine feminine heart of Lauryn Hill. Through Lauryn Hill's work one might liken her to the ancient Goddess Ma'at who stood for all that is good and righteous. Lauryn Hill, like Tupac, sang and rhymed about the problems of youth, but she did so with a more sensitive, womanly approach.

Art, like music, emanates out of African culture and is expressed through the spiritual soul. Sound is the result of vibratory sensations perceived by the sense of hearing, whereby auditory impressions are developed. Color and art, on the other hand, are the result of light splitting into different wavelengths, vibrating at different speeds and frequencies. Humans visualize and feel the vibrations of various color configurations. Cooper (1997) compiled art that could be seen through the sound of jazz. The vibratory sounds in this case were so sensitively intense and mixed with feelings of hurt, joy and love. The improvisational sound rhythms were constantly changed to produce various light wavelengths. These light wavelengths were repeatedly changing and vibrating at different speeds and frequencies and producing beautiful mixtures of color compositions. According to Barnes (1988), African people, by way of the melanin chemical in the body, are able to change sound energy to light energy and back again. Melanin allows one to open the third eye and perceive art in music and music in art.

African Americans must understand in both heart and soul that their rhythms in dance, music and art were developed with the desire to be in harmony with the one creative force. To reawaken the African mind, the movements in dance, the sounds in music and the color compositions in art must be understood from the old African perspective of harmony and balance. The old Africans saw this harmony and balance being achieved from duality. They felt that there was always a balancing of the various universal forces and that all the celestial bodies were in harmony and balance with each other. According to Hall (1998), Pythagoras determined that the vibrational movement of the universe creates perfect harmonious musical tones and colors. The old Africans knew that they were just a part of the creative plan of continuous regeneration. They felt connected to the one spiritual soul that creates matter from light. As a result, they danced, made sounds, and created beautiful art in an attempt to generate a vibrational state that would allow them to be one with the creator.

Today African people all over the world must go beyond money, power, and status in developing a definition of self. They must continue to dance, make music and create art. This will enable them to go deep into their African souls and commune with the ancestors through the eternal spirit of the cosmos, and know that the self is indestructibly connected in harmony and balance with the spirit of the creator in the circle of everlasting love.

Be skillfull in speech so that you succeed. The tongue of a man is his sword and effective speech is stronger than all fighting. None can overcome the skillful. A wise person is a school for the nobles and those who are aware of his knowledge do not attack him. No evil takes place when he is near. Truth comes to him in its essential form, shaped in the saying of the ancestors.

Taken from the Book of Kheti in Husia
Retranslated by Maulana Karenga

Similarities Between
Dr. Martin Luther King, Jr.'s Speeches and Tupac Shakur's Recordings in Rhythmic Spiritual Sound, Style and Intent (1999)

At first glance, to determine similarities between any of Dr. Martin Luther King Jr.'s speeches and Tupac Shakur's recordings would appear to be an impossible task. Most Americans, both Black and White, would find it utterly preposterous to attempt such a difficult task. Dr. King was perceived as one of the greatest Americans to have ever lived. He gave speeches that stirred one's soul and even made many White Americans reevaluate their moral and ethical positions. He was, without a doubt, the father of the Civil Rights Movement. On the other hand, Tupac was perceived as a thug and gangster rapper, who primarily touched the heart and soul of many inner city youth in ways that were astonishing to members of the Civil Rights generation. He often carried a gun and spent time in prison. Sometimes in his music, he expressed unadulterated anger and at other times unyielding love and care for young people in pain. On the surface these two men seem to be as different as day and night. But in reality, they both seem to have had a conscious vision that determined their powerful spiritual rhythmic styles.

Dr. Martin Luther King, Jr.'s rhythmic style was the result of his Christian background as a Baptist preacher. His style was most probably developed from his Black church experience and listening to Dr. Benjamin E. Mays every Tuesday morning in chapel while he was a student at Morehouse College. Dr. Mays, a scholar who had deep feelings about the plight of African Americans, had great oratorical skills. He probably had a most profound effect on the development of Dr. King's oratorical style as well as the deep spiritual feelings that were exhibited in his sermons. Most of Dr. King's speeches expressed an understanding of the pain that Black people were feeling as a result of living in a segregated society where African American children attended inferior schools; where White Colleges and Universities in the South were closed to Blacks; and where the primary jobs for Blacks were those of preaching, teaching, menial labor and racketeering. During his speeches, his voice rolled with a thundering sound as if all of the words were coming from God, expressing regret about the unethical inequalities and injustices that are endemic in American society.

His use of language was brilliant. He always chose the right parables or metaphors to make his points. In his "I Have a Dream" speech, his choice of words had such a spiritual driving force that many persons all over the nation, both Black and White, felt compelled to become more engaged in the nonviolent struggle for justice and freedom for African Americans.

Dr. King's "I Have a Dream" speech was one of the greatest speeches ever delivered. His wife, Mrs. Coretta Scott King, once commented, "at that moment it seemed as if the Kingdom of God appeared. But only lasted for a moment."It was as if the rhythm of his voice was in tune with the spiritual harmony of the cosmic universe. The vibrations of his voice penetrated the inner soul of most persons listening. They felt his Divine passion and immediately understood that this man had moved to the status of a prophet. His spiritual reality had transcended that of the average human being. He probably achieved what Finch (1998) called a quantum consciousness that allowed him to have Divine speech, where he was able to commune with the ancestors. In this case, through the spiritual penetration of his soul, he was also able to receive insights that are off limits to the ordinary person.

Tupac on the other hand, in his Makaveli recordings, seemed to have extended the idea of thug life to a new level. Tupac took the name "Makeveli" from a sixteenth-century Italian writer and statesman by the name of Niccolo Machiavelli whose chief writing was The Prince. In this book, he developed a systematic discourse on the methods by which a politician may cause his state to rise as a power. One of his most noted quotes was, "The end always justifies the means and it is safer to be feared than to be loved." According to Tupac, he idolized, not the man, but his thinking. This type of thinking was perhaps used by Tupac to place himself in a superior ego position to teach other rappers about the problems involved in living solely for money and prestige. Maybe he blasted Mobb Deep, Jay-Z, and Biggie to demonstrate how jealousy and envy could destroy friendships and continue to keep the African American community in turmoil; or maybe because of his own feelings of anger and revenge he blasted these rappers for falling prey to the same money, power, and status conscience that produced the behavior of many rappers.

In either case, Tupac produced rhythmic sounds that moved the internal being of most youth. He put words to their pain. The drug pushers, the crack heads and even those youths living in the inner city who were trying to do the right thing were moved by the raw realness of the human expressions in his music. For many persons of earlier generations, the language style and driving angry lyrics were intolerable and as a result they failed to comprehend the pain that he felt and why the youth of his generation could empathize with him so easily.

Tupac's oratorical style was not driven by typical middle class experiences like those of Dr. King, but probably by his love of the arts and his experience surviving on the streets. Subsequently, Tupac developed his oratorical style from rap music, an art form that started on the streets of New York City. His socially conscious lyrics were more than likely influenced by his mother's experiences as a member of the Black Panther Party. Like Dr. King, his love of reading, along with an extremely sensitive human nature, helped him acquire an oratorical style in rap music that caused young African Americans to relate to his musical sounds. These sounds made them feel alive and that someone understood what they were experiencing in their effort to survive. Often his lyrics and rhythmic sounds took on a strong air of defiance against a system that he felt did not care about its youth. These rhythms and rhymes in rap music always seemed to have come from what Tupac was feeling at the time. He chose the moment to share with the world what life was like for many young people. His language and rhythmic style were a rebellion against the normal societal behavioral standards but were loved and emulated by young people. Similar to Dr. King, but using a different oratorical technique, he forced many Americans to look at their own hypocrisy.

Dr. King and Tupac, typical of most African Americans, experienced what many African American psychologists call a double consciousness. Both struggled with the idea of what it meant to be Black living in America. Dr. King, while leading the struggle for the civil rights of African Americans, never dealt with the reality of the major differences between African culture and European culture to the extent that it was a primary factor in the development of the African American community. Dr. King seems to have been more comfortable with the idea of integrating into the larger European culture and attempting to make it more humane. Tupac, like Dr. King, felt that money would be a great equalizer. It appeared as if both believed that the lack of money was what kept African Americans trapped in despair. Dr. King and Tupac both had deep feelings and concerns about the plight of African Americans, but neither appeared to understand that money nor civil rights would ever empower all African Americans. Both seem to have had visions of money and power as the cure for all African people.

Even so, both were influenced by their African heritage in developing their oratorical styles. Their spiritual consciousness allowed them to project a spirit of sensitivity and caring. Both had the capacity to temporarily move away from their European indoctrinated consciousness of cold-hearted competition to the African collective conscience of love. This was a tremendous challenge for Tupac in that he had to overcome his disgust with how the American social and economic systems worked against young Black men. His African conscience had him on a serious mission of articulating through his music how social and economic systems were working to destroy young Black men. Sometimes he sounded, through his forceful and driving rhymes and rhythms, like he had left his body and was rhyming in harmony with the creator. But unfortunately, on other occasions, he would succumb to his European conscience of competition and Machiavellian power.

It appears that toward the end of Dr. King's life he became centered within himself. This was never more apparent than the night before he made his sermon that was entitled "I See the Promised Land." In that sermon he uttered the following words:

Well, I don't know what will happen now. We've got some difficult days ahead. But it doesn't matter with me now, because I've been to the mountaintop. And I don't mind. Like anybody, I would like to live a long life. Longevity has its place. But I'm not concerned about that now. I just want to do God's will. And He's allowed me to go up to the mountain. And I've looked over. And I've seen the promised land. I may not get there with you. But I want you to know tonight, I'm not worried about anything. I'm not fearing any man. Mine eyes have seen the glory of the coming of the Lord.

It seemed, in this sermon, that for the first time he was centered within himself. He knew that he was going to die. He understood that he had become too powerful. Pepper (1995) explained convincingly that there were orders to kill Dr. King and that the major players were the National Security Agency (NSA), the CIA, the FBI, and the Office of Naval Intelligence. Considering Dr. King's tremendous influence over the Civil Rights movement, coupled with his pronouncement that the United States' participation in the Vietnam War was immoral, placed him in the position, as seen by U.S. Government Officials, of being a threat to national security. Pepper (1995) inferred that the times were of such in 1968 that Dr. King had to be killed.

Dr. King's knowledge of the coming of his own death gave him what appeared to be apocalyptic insight. His last sermon was delivered with a style and rhythm as if God was guiding his thoughts. The oratorical style and rhythmic tones of his voice reverberated throughout the Bishop Charles Mason Temple in Memphis, Tennessee. It is no doubt in my mind that the tones that he created entered the ear and activated the nervous system of each person present. The spirit, as a result, moved up and down the whole body of everyone. Those persons present probably also felt that he was going to die, but they further felt that this man was moving toward immortality, understanding that they could kill his body, however, the brave spirit from which the beautiful rhythmic spiritual tones came would live forever.

It is ironic that both Dr. King and Tupac had a premonition about their own death. Tupac made many songs where he spoke of his death. It was as if he understood that he was exerting too much influence on the behavior of young Black men. This influence was growing by leaps and bounds. Many of these Black men were carrying guns and were being educated about the ill effects of the American social and economic systems in the Black community. Several of his recordings used the slogan "I'm a soldier." Other rappers were beginning to use these words as well. It would be interesting to know what the CIA and FBI were thinking while listening to these songs. Were they concerned about his ability to excite many young Black men with guns and that one day they might be a threat to national security?

Tupac had foresight that most people missed. He wanted to bring young Black men together to build their own positive resources for the good of the community. He further wanted young Black men to get past their jealousy and envy and pool their energies to help all the little brothers and sisters who were on the streets struggling on their own with no choices but to turn to drugs as a way of survival. While Tupac wanted to accomplish many worthwhile things for the Black community, his personal internal conflicts with himself, problems that he created with some of his peers, and the threading messages that he sent out in his music made him keenly aware that his death was imminent.

Tupac's awareness that death was nearing drove him to accomplish as much as he could in a small length of time. As a consequence, he made recordings after recordings. Like Dr. King, Tupac, knowing that death was approaching, did some of his best work. His song entitled, "Resist the Temptation," suggests that he had become centered with his spiritual self. In this song, Tupac very compassionately spelled out the feelings and life of a drug user. He empathetically explained the horror in the life of a drug user, and how their children suffered. He also reminded us that someone at the top of the social and economic system was getting rich off of the misery of Black drug users.

Tupac seemed to have expanded his awareness to a new horizon. His perceptions were of such magnitude that he was able to see through the generations of African Americans' brainwashing, and intuitively discern the true reality of what was good and what was bad in the African American community. This instinctive awareness lead him to record another song entitled "Unconditional Love." In this song, he described a clear picture of what unconditional love really meant. He enlightens us to the fact that through all our trials and tribulations, a love that is in harmony with the creator is always abiding and continuous.

Tupac not only wrote songs, but he was an excellent poet. He wrote one poem that perhaps gives one a real glimpse into his soul. The poem is entitled "In the Event of MY Demise." In this poem he states that:

In the event of my Demise
when my heart can beat no more
I Hope I Die FOR A Principle
or A Belief that I had Lived 4
I will die Before MY TIME
Because I feel the shadow's Depth
so much I wanted 2 accomplish
before I reach my Death

I have come 2 grips with the possibility
and wiped the last tear from My eyes
I Loved ALL who were Positive
In the event of my Demise

The greatness of both Dr. King and Tupac Shakur was tempered by a spiritual force that heighten their conscientiousness. This enabled them to open what the ancient African called the third eye. In this case, they were able to envision the one source of universal energy. This one source controlled the sounds that came from their voices. It empowered them with the knowledge of duality. They understood that the universe is always expanding, contracting and regenerating every second in time. This understanding compelled both of them to listen to the left brain hemisphere of the ancient Black Egyptian god Tehuti, who was the brilliant logical thinker. Dr. King and Tupac were also influenced by the right brain hemisphere of the ancient goddess Ma'at who brought forth the feelings of love, compassion, righteousness, and justice.

Dr. King and Tupac lived during different times. Dr. King's energy was directed toward Civil Rights and Tupac's in describing the real life of many young African Americans living in the inner city. But the rhythmic sounds that came from their voices were similar in that they each were able to express, through their voices, a consciousness that allowed them to feel and experience the past, keenly view their role in the present, and move into the future in harmony with the creator. While their stature in the African American community was different, Dr. King, a minister and civil rights leader, and Tupac, a rapper and actor, both, through their diverse oratorical styles, heard the cries of millions of Africans who died during the middle passage and all those

African Americans who have died since. They heard the African drums that were in rhythm with the heartbeat of all those Africans and placed their heartbeats in unison with those brave brothers and sisters. So, for them to walk into hell for a just cause was easy. They knew that the spirit of all those Africans who died was with them. Both Dr. King and Tupac walked to their death in the spirit of universal love with the one intent of being able to say, I did my best to create a more humane and just America for African American people.

The rhythmic spiritual sounds of Dr. King and Tupac were different. Their styles were different. But the intent of their hearts was the same. The styles of both were influenced by their African cultural heritage. This culture began with the spirit and continues with a soulful rhythm. They both, while on earth, struggled to be in harmony with the spirit of Ma'at and today they are home living in harmony with the ever moving universal cosmic spirit.

When Ra emerged in his Barque for the first time and creation came into being, he was standing on the pedestal of Ma'at. Thus the Creator, Ra, lives by Ma'at and has established Creation on Ma'at. Who is Ma'at? Ma'at represents the very order which constitutes creation. Therefore, it is said that Ra created the universe by putting Ma'at in the the place of chaos. So creation itself is Ma'at. Creation without order is chaos. Ma'at is profound teaching in reference to the nature of creation and the manner in which human conduct should be cultivated. It refers to a deep understanding of Divinity and the manner in which virtuous qualities can be developed in the human heart so as to come closer to the divine.

Ma'at is a Philosophy, a spiritual symbol as well as a cosmic energy or force which pervades the entire universe. She is the symbolic embodiment of world order, justice, righteousness, correctness, harmony and peace. She is also known by her headdress composed of a feather of truth. She is a form of the goddess Aset, who represents wisdom and spiritual awakening through balance and equanimity.

Taken from The Wisdom of Ma'at by Muata Ashby

Kemetic Principles of Ma'at and Tehuti: A Blueprint for African Male - Female Relationships (2001)

The Kemetic principles of Ma'at and Tehuti are profoundly important as a blueprint for African male- female relationships. These concepts symbolize the moral and ethical foundation of early African society. This view of relationships was based on nature's rule of duality that governs all cosmic phenomena. According to the Kemetic Book of Coming Forth by Day, "Ra," who was the sun God at the time of creation, was assisted by his daughter, Ma'at. Ma'at, as an aspect of the creator, represented the female principle that was characterized by seven cardinal virtues of human perfectibility: truth, justice, propriety, harmony, balance, reciprocity and order. The male aspect of creation was represented by Tehuti, the husband of Ma'at. Tehuti was the neter that denoted the higher consciousness of wisdom and interpreted the cosmic mind of the creator. When these dual cosmic features of "Ra" work together in harmony and balance, universal order is the result. In this case, the rhythm of the human body and mind is in sync with the cosmos and the consequence is excellent physical and mental health, the prerequisite for good male-female relationships.

Equally important to maintaining healthy male-female relationships is understanding the rhythm of Ma'at and Tehuti in their harmonious marriage. The body cannot exist without the aspects of both Ma'at and Tehuti. It is impossible for the flesh of the body to live if both the male aspect (Tehuti) and the female aspect (Ma'at) are not working together harmoniously. The cells of the body are able to stay alive through the complementary vibratory movement of its component parts. These polarized vibratory movements occur as a result of the cause and effect action in the production of energy. Similarly, the physical sun reflects off the moon creating the gravitational and vibrational interaction of all celestial bodies. These interactions are guided by the resulting spiritual consciousness of the one creator. Ma'at and Tehuti, in Kemetic thought, were reflections of the consciousness of the Sun God, "Ra." The harmony and balance between Ma'at and Tehuti were necessary in order to continue the creative cycle. Inside this cycle, the wisdom of the one creator was manifested in Tehuti. It is through the wisdom of Tehuti that Ma'at embodies the standards that govern human behavior.

Ma'atian principles represent a model of how the sun, moon and all celestial bodies work together. Ma'at demands that all universal movements, whether physical or social, are purposeful. The purpose must be in keeping with universal order. In the case of physical body movements, when the movements are in rhythm with the sounds of various creative configurations of the cosmos, the result is poetry in motion. When social behavior is guided by purpose, the result is a loving, sensitive and caring attitude. The principle of Ma'at created universal order and helped humans understand that everything in the cosmos is connected to everything else.

According to Adams (1994), the Ma'atian principle conceived order in every imaginable fashion, "from the cosmic order of the rhythm of the sun, moon, planets and stars to the social order of man and woman, caregivers and children, state and society, music and poetry," and referred to both balance and harmony as necessary to develop the aesthetic sensibility to enjoy the beauty of music, art, color, and rhythm. Compassion was a natural outgrowth of the expression of this sensibility and inspired happiness and affection toward other human beings. Essential to understanding the principle of Ma'at is having a sense of its ecological foundation, found in the virtue of reciprocity. Reciprocity recognizes the harmonious complementarity and interdependence of all forms of life. It explains the necessary partnership between men and women, children and their families, and the community and the elders. The acceptance of this virtue helps one to know that everything that goes around does come back around. This is observed in the reality that there is a spiritual force that keeps everything moving and regenerating every millisecond in time. Cognizance of these virtues is an absolute requirement for individuals to practice truth and justice. In Kemetic philosophy all persons were judged on the final scale of justice to determine if they had lived by the virtues of Ma'at.

The problem with African American male-female relationships today is that the connection between what might be termed the Ma'atian right brain and Tehutian left brain has become disoriented. Consequently, African men and women have problems bonding with their own souls. African men are locked into the European competitive macho mentally. Sensitive men are perceived as weak. In this case men are not supposed to cry; only women cry. According to Chandler (1999), "The vision of why men are on earth, which is contained in the feminine mind, is muddled with aggression, arrogance, and insensitivity." Unfortunately, women are forced to live in a patriarchal culture where they are constantly fighting for greater expressions of equality. This fight forces them to consistently engage in the more aggressive male-oriented patterns of survival behavior.

The problem is magnified if one partner is struggling to reclaim his or her African mind and the other is not. The competition between them is then forced to a new level. The struggle of one partner to maintain the European value system of individuality, independence and the survival of the fittest mentality becomes more pronounced. The African value system that featured groupness, cooperation, collective responsibility, interdependence and one with nature is difficult for this person because of fear and the inability to commune with their own soul. The idea of Ma'at and Tehuti, being aspects of the one creator, is impossible for them to comprehend. The African American male and female are usually driven by their developed European nature of competition and ego satisfaction. The African, unlike the European, wanted to live close to nature. More specifically, the African wanted to be one with nature. The nature of the European created the desire to control nature rather than to live in harmony and balance with the rhythms of the universe. As a result, Europeans failed to develop a feeling and understanding of all the possible spiritual universal rhythms. They could not feel the deep vibrations of the soul. Their body cells did not allow them to develop a deep awareness of the spiritual harmonic vibrations of the soul. They were only familiar with a few combinations of cell vibrations. They never moved their bodies to the many possible movements, or listened to the many universal sounds, or saw the many possibilities of colors. They never knew that there was a direct connection between heaven and the human body. The early Africans were aware of how the total body was fashioned like the universe. They knew that the same oxygen, carbons, hydrogen, and nitrogen that are in the sun also create human energy and ultimately preserve life. They knew that through conscious moving spirit, the cell of the human body would continue to be rejuvenated. They understood that human cells without conscious spirit could not live.

Therefore, they worked hard to develop the spiritual self through experiencing the various vibrations of harmony and balance between their souls and the one soul. They came to realize that through the body's endocrine system, it was possible to feel and know things beyond one's daily reality. Through deep thought, the Africans discerned that the pineal gland, if fully functional, would enable them to experience movement patterns, hear sounds and perceive colors as a result of the opening of what they referred to as the third eye, "the all seeing Eye of Horus."

African American men and women must be centered in the one cosmic rhythmic circle from birth to rebirth with the understanding that it is the conscience of the one creator that holds all matter together. The self is then an extension of the conscience of the one creator who is both male (Tehuti) and female (Ma'at) at the same time. So then, in the creative process, when the mother and father move their bodies together in rhythm with the cosmos, it is in keeping with the creators conscious dynamic energy flow, the same spiritual energy that moves the universe. When the beautiful movements of the mother and father reach orgasmic perfection, with the protons, neurons and electrons that make up both the male and female consciousness unit together, cosmic harmony is increased. This increased conscious energy insures the continuous harmony and balance of the spiritual soul from death to rebirth. The spiritual cycle continues.

One can only imagine what beautiful rhythmic movements and sounds African people will make when Putah merges with all the other dimensions of the soul in the circle of cosmic order; when the body, mind, and spirit are in rhythmical harmony and balance with the soul of the creator. The Africans will then be healthy again, making music and moving in rhythmic harmony and balance all the time, not being influenced by European thought and behavior. They will be guided by the wisdom of Tehuti and the soulful sensitivity of Ma'at. They will always then experience the harmony of cosmic order.

The Kamites used numbers in an effort to express the importance of duality and to comprehend the circle of cosmic harmony and order. According to Lubicz (1978), they used numbers to create the order needed to understand their existence. He felt that they believed that it was only through an insight into numbers that one could express the continued creation of the universe; and that the individual self was simply a part of the spiritual energy that regenerated the rebirth of everything.

The Kamites understood that everything is in everything. Consequently, the number "1" represented creation as it pointed upward toward the sun and downward toward water. Both the sun and water working together represented duality, the principle of opposites that provided the ultimate source for all life. In this case the sun God, "Ra", gives off hydrogen and oxygen to produce water. This water is held on earth by the moon's gravitational pull. The Kamites knew that between the two opposite poles from heaven to earth, water is evaporated by the sun to produce clouds. Hence, clouds develop between the sun and earth and at the right temperature there is rain. There is a continuous reciprocal response between rain from heaven and water evaporation from earth. The Kamites saw this as the union of two opposites in the regenerative process. Symbolically, they placed two lines together, one at the base representing water, the other pointing toward the sun and moon and in their infinite wisdom, placed a third line that closed the space in absolute unity and formed a right triangle. The triangle portrayed the three fold nature of Divinity. As a result, the first Immaculate Conception Story was born with Asaru (Osiris) representing the masculine principle and Aset (Isis), representing the female principle, while the connecting side of the triangle represented the child, Heru (Horus).

The number "4" illustrated their realization that for harmony and balance to exist in human matter, there must be a connecting source. Consequently, the square emerged with four equal sides in perfect balance. The addition of the fourth line gave matter a spiritual energized soul that led to their intuitive perception of universal order and rhythm. The number "5" allowed them to accentuate the five senses and perceive the essence of what it felt like to live and move in concert with the rhythm of the Creator. The senses in humans are what draws the male and female together. In the nature of things, one is incomplete without the other. It was the number "6" that provoked harmony in duality that stimulated the merger of complementary opposites to ensure that all creatures on earth and elsewhere continued the process of rebirth.

The Kamites felt that the number "7" was the most mystical of all the numbers. This was the number that gave energy to the soul. It was the ultimate force that integrated the cosmic universe. It is also the force that keeps the human heart beating and the melatonin secreting from the pineal gland. These phenomenons allow humans to experience the inner spiritual world. During the orgasm between the male and female when the male sperm enters the female egg, both spirit and matter come together and life begins to form.

The number "8" enhanced the ability to expand outward and have a multitude of cosmic experiences. Heaven, to the Kamites, was a vast place as is the human body. They symbolically placed one zero on top of the other showing that the human body is connected to the universal body, and in each complete circle the expansion and contraction keep cosmic movement in absolute order.

The number "9" represented the completion of a cycle and the return to the original source or origin. Human death is certain, but so is life. The male and female will always lay down together to perform the sacred act of sex. The sex drive is profound and when the male and female are equally involved in a caring and loving relationship, at the moment of the orgasm, they are able to, for that time, experience the soul of the other and through spirit, commune with the soul of the creator. The circle of death and rebirth is forever and will never stop. It will always move with the energetic spiritual soul as a collective oneness.

For African men and women to develop a genuine sense of self, it is necessary to understand the relationship between the celestial process and the human process. The evolution of the mind, body and soul are fashioned like the heavens in perfect harmony and balance. Individuals should not just live in a linear mind world, but must strive to unify the right and left brain functions so that compassion, truth, justice and love become a way of life. The over emphasis on money, power and status will destroy African male-female relationships. Money and power are important for survival of the African people as a group. But for the African family to survive African men must become as wise as Tehuti and take care of their women. Women, on the other hand, must be more sensitive and caring. Only then, with African men and women coming together in rhythmic cosmic harmony, will the African Americans be whole again and take their rightful place in bringing leadership to the world. The creator has given African Americans a special gift. It is time to use it by balancing the lower and the upper self and looking toward the light of "Ra." It is in the power of the circle of the light that the principles of Tehuti and Ma'at are perfected. African men must be in tune with the mind of Tehuti and African women with the soul of Ma'at fully knowing that matter only comes into existence through the energy created by thought. The African man and woman must be mindful of the fact that matter, whether plant or human, follow the same geometric blueprint at creation. When a human birth occurs, the male spasm reaches and penetrates the ovum and conception commences.

According to Chandler (1999), "the events that lead up to conception are extremely noteworthy in dramatizing a universal rebirth." He suggests that "when that one chosen sperm penetrates the ovum, its tail breaks off, and its head forms a sphere the same size as the female pro nucleus. These two merge, forming a perfect blueprint for all universal knowledge." The sperm and ovum pass through one another creating the first cell identification as the human zygote, containing forty-four chromosomes. Mitosis then occurs where opposite or polar bodies are created that travel to opposite ends of the cell nodes, forming northern and southern polarities. The zygote then splits into four cells and later eight cells, and a star tetrahedron is developed with these eight cells lying directly under the center cell. The resulting geometric symbol that is created by the interaction of the male sperm and the female ovum represents universal creation.

African men and women must reflect on Kemetic symbolisms that characterize the heavens above as the female goddess "Nut" and earth as the male god "Geb" with "Shu" the air that separates heaven and earth, creating a physical world and a heavenly world, where the wound of "Nut" in the creative process is always ready to receive the penis of

"Geb". In this case, the female goddess "Nut" and the male god "Geb" represents the male and female principles of creation. This continuous reuniting of heaven and earth keeps the universe moving in harmony and balance with the mind of the creator. If one considers the female vagina to be heaven and the male penis to be earth, it is impossible for one to do without the other. It is just the nature of universal order. The blueprint of the creators' soul is within us. Let's merge the two and always make love in cosmic rhythmic harmony with the wisdom of Tehuti and intense caring of Ma'at.

As you watch people dance, focus on them and their movements. The movements are reflections of the forces coming to them and through them. Observe, and absorb the rhythms their bodies are making. It is "the gods" talking. Listen with your eyes.

When you observe, you can intuit and ingest energy from the dances and know which of their motions needs to be accented. Then you can give the energy right back to them. In his book The Healing Drum, Yaya Diallo speaks of recognizing disharmonies in people's spirits by observing their dancing. He, or his teachers, would then switch the rhythm around to help the person out. I wish everyone knew this. There's almost nothing more painful for a dancer than to be beat down with the music when it is supposed to be taking them up higher.

Taken from The Drummer's Path by Sule Greg Wilson

African American Movement Patterns in Sports and Dance:
A Function of Kametic Cosmology
(2002)

African American movement patterns in sports and in dance are a wonder to behold. It is like watching poetry in motion. In sports, athletes move with such grace and effortless beauty. Basketball players are able to move with speed and at the same time change direction at will. They can dribble with both hands, and between both legs without missing a beat. They can glide in air, and defy physical mechanical principles, by changing directions before landing on their feet. While shooting a twenty or thirty-foot jump shoot, their depth perception is often uncanny. They are able to calculate the distance between their hands and the basket and send an accurate message over their neuromuscular system without missing any clues. Similarly, football players move with tremendous speed and catch passes using acrobatic moves in air. Good running backs intuitively see small openings and move through space with flawless movements like ballet dancers.

African American dancers create movement patterns that are both beautiful and complicated. From hip-hop to ballet, the movements are intriguing. African Americans seem to be able to move their bodies in many planes and around many axes. They are able to move their arms, hips, trunk and legs in so many different rhythms and patterns so that new movements are continuously being created and recreated. In both hip-hop and ballet, African Americans are able to perfect complicated polyrhythmic movements.

One might wonder what sports, music and dance would

be like in the United States of America without the influence of African Americans. Consider what the National Basketball Association was like during the 1950's before African Americans were allowed to play. Basketball games were very slow and methodical. All the movements were in pre-designed patterns. There was little rhythm or creativity in the movements. The game was reminiscent of the stiff German military march. The players preformed movements that were rigid and without grace and aesthetic beauty.

Similarly, in the European culture, symphony music and ballet were perceived as elegant and beautiful, but to most African Americans they seemed to be constrained and without spontaneity. The movements in each were stiff and exact. To make music and movements that projected complicated rhythms of human love, caring, and suffering seemed to be difficult. The symphony music was full of what appeared to be sounds of war, booming storms, and hard struggles, not sounds that expressed human sensitive feelings.

African Americans, on the other hand, have been able, to some extent, to hold on to their spiritual souls. It appears that through struggles Africans were able to intensify their feelings and maintain an awareness of universal rhythms. African Americans used those intense feeling and their rhythmic spiritual awareness to excel in sports and dance. For example, athletes like Michael Jordan and Allen Iverson do things with a basketball that show an uncanny sense of kinesthetic awareness. Their movements are often beyond belief. These athletes have superior depth perception and visual acuity. As a result, they are able to envision everything that is happening around them on the basketball court and respond with precision to the specific situation. They also have the ability, probably because of their pineal gland and their melaninated cell, to send impulses over the sensory neurons to the motor neurons and have them appropriately interpreted at the synaptical gap or neuromuscular junction. This interpretation enables them to perceive rhythms that are both internal and external.

This spiritual experience, it appears, opens the door to the many universal rhythms of the human body and those of trees and flowers. For a brief moment in time they appear to be in contact with the rhythms of the creator by way of their own souls. During these times their movements seem to be in harmony with cosmic forces. As a result, all body cells function in tune with the universal consciousness of duality. In turn, their bodies move like the beautiful rhythms in a colorful piece of art or like the rhythms in a brilliant jazz composition played by John Coltrane.

African American women, in many cases, bring the concept of Ma'at into sports. Venus Williams and her sister Serena move their bodies with the grace and harmony of a beautiful, colorful butterfly when they stroke the tennis ball. They move with the strength of "Ra" and with the fluid and aesthetic motions of Ma'at. Their hand and eye coordination, peripheral vision, and reaction time is extraordinary. Similar to African American basketball players, their sensory neurons receive the appropriate impulses or messages and send them across the synaptical gaps at the neuromuscular junction where they are perfectly interpreted at a phenomenal rate of speed and sent to the motor neurons to allow for their graceful picturesque movements on the tennis court. The speed of these impulses across the neuromuscular junction is the result of their melaninated cells creating a fast polarization of the neurons. This polarization is reminiscent of the relationship between the Kemetic female Ma'atian principle and the male Tehutian principle. This process of duality enables them to guide across the tennis court in perfect harmony and balance with a keen sense of the reciprocity between their bodies, the tennis rackets and the tennis balls. This temporary intense Ma'atian cosmic awareness enables them to be in rhythm with cosmic order, calculate the speed and direction of the tennis balls, and to kinesthetically know where all their body parts are in space.

African Americans have used the sound and cosmic rhythms of their African heritage to create many new movements in all sports and dances. In boxing, when Muhammad Ali first beat Sonny Liston, every American thought that this was impossible. However, when they began to watch the beauty of his steps, his circular and intricate dance movements, and his ability to quickly move his body at various angles to absolve the blows of his opponents, they knew that Muhammad Ali had developed more than the normal one or two steps forward or backward and the usual one-two punch of most boxers, but had internalized the cosmic rhythms of an African American jazz musician. His hands, feet, hips and shoulders were all moving to the graceful polyrhymic tunes with many possible notes being played in one orderly measure. Sometimes the rhythmic one-two beats would be slow. But at other times the rhythmic three-four or four-four beats in punch combinations would be so fast the likes of Sonny Liston would not know what hit him. Muhammad Ali probably really had the cosmic vision of being able to "float like a butterfly and sting like a bee," moving quickly and lightly through air in harmony and balance.

It was not just in boxing that African Americans expressed their cosmic rhythmic consciousness but in tap dance as well. During the early slave trade in America when the fearful slaveholders in the South would not allow the Africans to use the drum, they started to tap out complex rhythmic passages with their feet. By the mid-nineteenth century, after being influenced by Irish and British one-two beat clogging, African Americans created what has become multi-rhythmic tap dancing. With their feet they beat out the rhythms of the drum.

Today, Gregory Hines calls the young brother, Savion Glover, the finest tapper of all times. According to Savion, he taps to the beats that naturally come to him. He is not so interested in style but the rhythms that just come to him. Savion is able to beat out the rhythms of the African drum or create fully developed melodies and harmonies with the swinging of his hips and the tapping of his feet. Much like the rapper Tupac Shakur, Savion expresses a wide range of feelings and complicated rhythms. Savion produces tap rhythmic rhymes with his tap dancing that express the hip-hop generation's joy, sorrow, pride and anger. Savion appears to be able to hear the natural beats of his own heart and connect with the expansion and contraction of the universe. Similar to Muhammad Ali, Savion is able to hear many cosmic rhythms. As a result, he is able to tap to the sometimes complex and intricate jazz rhythms, and to the often hard, angry and perplexing rhythms of the hip-hop culture. In each case, he seems to always be trying to experience the one spiritual force that determines all possible tapping movements that may be created.

African Americans have listened to the Kemetic Khaba part of their soul and transformed sports, music and dance in America. According to Malone (1996), movement is life to African Americans. She maintains that their cosmic reality is stored in the brain and is seen in all phases of African American life. From Florida A&M University's band putting African dance into their marching routine to Black Colleges' sororities and fraternities stepping and developing precise, sharp and complex rhythmical body movements combined with singing, chanting and verbal play. Always, African Americans are creating and revolutionizing the rhythms in the American culture.

The time has come for African Americans to fuse all parts of the soul together. The Kemetic Khaba part of the soul is complete. African Americans must continue to strive to go beyond the five senses to move in absolute concert with the rhythmic power of the creator. African Americans must use the true sixth sense, through their melanized cells, and move to the Kemetic Putah intellectual part of the soul and fuse with the Kemetic Atum, the most Devine part of the soul, to envision the continuous merger of complementary opposites in the many rhythms in the circle from birth, to death, and rebirth. Once this merger is completed, one can only imagine what new movements African Americans will create in sports and dance, or more importantly, how then will African Americans influence the world culture.

Het-Heru's (Hathor) temples were often healing centers, such as Het-Heru's main shrine at Dendera, where all manner of therapies were practiced, just like a hospital in our modern sense, more or less, but with more emphasis on healing the body and soul using all means and not limited to surgical procedures.

Het-Heru represents the intimate relationship between music, dance, and the well-being of people.

To heal a person is to restore the inner balance, by bringing that person back into tune. Music and dance are sometimes needed, in conjunction with medical and surgical procedures.

Music, singing, chanting, and dancing generate sonar fields, and soundwaves are now utilized more and more in surgical procedures. There are different types of soundwaves that can be used for different purposes. An example is the ultra-soundwaves, which cannot be detected by our ears, but doctors use its power as a kind of knifeless scalpel in microsurgery.

The voice generate soundwaves that can have similar impacts on the vibratory system of the bodily organs. The vocal powers should not and cannot be underestimated. Witness the powerful voice of the soprano singer, who can shatter a glass with her voice.

Incantation and poetic chanting are scientifically controlled soundwaves that generate sonar fields, establishing an immediate vibratory identity with the essential principle that underlies any object or form. By pronouncing certain words or names of power, in the proper manner and in the proper tone of voice, a priest/doctor can heal the sick.

Taken from Egyptian Rhythm by Moustafa Gadalla

Similarities Between African Sounds and Movements in Brazilian Capoeira and African American Hip Hop (2003)

The sounds and movements in Brazilian Capoeira and Hip Hop are quite different in their intent but both have their foundations deeply rooted in ancient African culture. The beautiful sounds and movements in Capoeira are either an art form brought from West Africa by slaves who were brought to Brazil by the Portuguese or developed in Brazil by Africans as a survival technique. In either case, the sounds and movements are purely African. Similarly, the sounds and movements in Hip Hop music and dance are solely African. Unfortunately, many older Americans view hip hop as a negative art form developed by African American youths. While it is true that Hip Hop sounds and movements were developed by African American youths, its rhythmic foundation has a spiritual dynamic that is rooted in ancient African cosmology.

African people, because of their rich cultural environmental sensitivity, were able to hear sounds of various birds, view the quickness of the cheetah and the graceful movements of the lion- the Africans heard and observed all the sounds and movements of other animals. They also were keenly aware of the behavior and communication methods of the plants and animals around them. Unlike the Europeans, the ancient Africans showed respect for all of creation.

The practice of Brazilian Capoeira as a means of self defense grew out of the need to survive the greed and barbarism of Europeans. It is estimated that between 1500 and 1900 about four million Africans crossed the Atlantic in disease-ridden Portuguese ships. These African people were from such countries as Nigeria, Angola, Benin and Mozambique and, upon arrival, continued to hear the cultural rhythmic beats of their homeland and created songs and dances. It is believed that the Africans taken to Brazil developed Capoeira from the traditional ritual dances done in their homelands in Africa and developed Capoeira to train the mind and body for combat situations. The dance ritual was cloaked in the guise as innocent-looking recreational dance.

Capoeira provided the Africans a means to endure the hardships of slavery and the ability to master a method of self-defense to fight for their freedom. Through cultural memory, they continued their strong spiritual, emotional songs and dances. According to Almieda (1986), the African slave developed a one string instrument called the "berimbau." This instrument was created to be used when playing Capoeira. He further made the point that the:

> Berimbau can pacify the soul when played in melancholy solos; the rhythm is Black and strong, a deep and powerful pulse that reaches the heart. It inundates the mind, space, and time with the intensity of an ocean tide. The dense aura that emanates from the single musical bow slowly envelops you. Without you realizing it, the powerful magic of the berimbau tames your soul.

The music and dance in Capoeira seem to awaken the ancestral spirits, allowing the Capoeiristas to move their bodies to deeper levels of rhythmic possibilities. The conscious focus is beyond their material existence, but is more in tune with the harmony of their natural surroundings.

The early Africans always had the desire to be in rhythmical harmony with the creative forces of the universe.

It is often difficult for older African Americans to hear and understand the African rhythmic beats in Hip Hop. Just as with performing the movements in Capoeira, the movements and beats come from the deep consciousness that is inherent in African cultural heritage. African American youths took the rhythms from gospel, jazz, and rhythm and blues to create a new rhythmic reality. The experience of developing rhymes to a rhythmic beat gives African American youths a means of expressing their hardships, social injustices, and also feeling of love. Sometimes the lyrics and rhythmic beats are hard, with expressions of violence and drug use, while at other times they express poetic themes of love and caring for their brothers and sisters and social injustices.

Capoeira and Hip Hop appear to be expressions through the African spiritual soul to be free. Both offer an opportunity to discover oneself by experiencing the rhythms of universal order. However, frequently Hip Hop artists are bound by their European consciousness and produce music that exploit the human unconscious propensity to engage in recreational sex and to commit unconscionable violent acts. But at other times artists like Hill produce music where she just simply shares her soul with the listener. In her struggle to remove herself from the European control of seeking fame and money; she digs deep into her African consciousness through her music. Through the spiritual and soulful rhythms that she is able to produce, her mind is opened to the reality of the destruction that is contained in European competition and greed. Her African Kametic Ma'atian self emerges and enables her to make a clear analysis of the system that created her personal disharmony.

On Lauryn Hill's CD, "Un-Plugged", she raps one song

entitled "Mystery of Iniquity" with profound intensity and a thorough understanding of how customs, mores, folkways, and institutions emerge. Her recitation in rhythmic rhyme is clearer for young African Americans and more descriptive of the hypocrisy and contradictions in America's social and economic systems than any Harvard doctoral graduate could have developed. In this one song, she takes us on the same journey that Marimba Ani does in her book entitled, Yurugu: An African-Centered Critique of European Cultural Thought and Behavior. Marimba explains in what she calls the European "Asili", that their cultural core lacked spiritual substance. Lauryn Hill in no uncertain terms explains how this European lack of spirit manifests itself in all of the United States' social and political institutions.

Another Hip Hop artist who goes by the names of Nas explains how America's social and economic systems negatively affect African Americans in the inner city. Many of the lyrics on his CD entitled *God's Son* are spell-bounding for African Americans who really care about African children. Like Tupac Shakur, he explains the struggles that children experience and how the thugs' life emerges with violence and drugs. He further explains that many children are on the streets without a father or mother to guide and provide love and care for their well-being. But, like Tupac, he also includes lyrics that express love for his mother and his appreciation for what she has done for him with few financial resources.

It is interesting and disturbing that both Capoeira and Hip Hop developed and grew as a result of poor African people struggling to survive. According to Chvasicer (2002), Capoeira, at one time in Rio de Janeiro, was viewed as merely a game (jogo) played by African slaves. But what appeared to be an innocent game with African ritual took on a war-like dance with high kicks performed in a circle that resembled martial arts. With these beautiful but dangerous dance movements, African slaves mounted an offense against their slave masters. The songs that were sung during the Capoeira dance movements were often songs of freedom. Participation in Capoeira appeared to be the place where Africans could continue, in the midst of captivity, to dance to the rhythmic sounds of their homeland and at the same time prepare for battle against their captors. The rhythms of the berimbau in Capoeira gave fuel to the African soul to move and develop physical endurance, muscular strength, and mental and emotional focus.

In Brazil today, like in the United States, slavery has been abolished, but institutional racism is stronger than ever. Also, like in the United States a large preponderance of African people are relegated to the bottom of the socioeconomic ladder. In Salvador Bahia, where a large number of people of African descent are located, Capoeira is still going strong. While Capoeira has changed and has many forms today, the game, dance or martial arts form in Bahia still has maintained its African foundation. Capoeira and Hip Hop represent the heart and soul of African people trying to exist in a European dominated culture where money, power and status are of paramount importance. Both Capoeira and Hip Hop were born out of the deep well of African consciousness, that is, in direct opposition to European ideology. The philosophy of putting a price on land and believing that time is money was foreign to the Africans. This concept made it almost impossible for Africans to adjust to the European way of life. In this type of environment one must earn money and own property to survive. Since Europeans had contrived to steal the land and money, and enslave human beings, they controlled most of the money and had the power to determine the distribution of all property and goods. For

African people, this was a catastrophic situation that often resulted in African people committing criminal acts in an effort to survive.

Unfortunately, in the struggle to survive, both Capoeira and Hip Hop developed a violent element that, on occasion, presented a problem for the society at large. In the case of Capoeira, Chvaicer (2002) in his article The Criminalization of Capoeira , pointed out that in Rio de Janeiro in the mid-1850s, public authorities reported that Capoeiristas often attacked innocent citizens for no reason. He further cited the fact that some citizens saw Capoeiristas "as dangerous criminals who were a serious threat not only to the public but also to the government due to their organization into violent and aggressive gangs. The chief of police noted that the Capoeiristas formed a sort of association, divided by neighborhoods, with specific leaders. They not only battled among themselves but also injured and murdered innocent passersby"(p. 531). The public authorities in Rio de Janeiro seemed to have been more concerned about the fact that a large majority of Capoeiristas were Black Africans who had been forced to the lower strata of society. The Brazilian White society was so afraid of the Capoeiristas that in 1890 they enacted a law to stop the Capoeiristas from performing. This law created a conflict between the public authorities and the lower classes. This conflict was readily seen during festivals and holidays when the Capoeiristas continued to play with their friends demonstrating their agility, flexibility and dance skills at public squares, entertaining the crowds who actively participated with hand clapping, songs and music. They continued to perform Capoeira in defiance of the ruling class.

The young African American Hip Hop generation has rejected the hypocrisy of the United States moral and ethical systems; and like the Capoeiristas during the 1800s who made accusations of injustice against the ruling class, many Rap Artists have denounced the American system as unjust, racist, and morally corrupt. The Hip Hop artists "dead prez" in their CD entitled "Lets get free" explained in no uncertain terms, in their songs, like "Police State," Behind Enemy Lines and "Assassination," how they feel about how African people are treated in the United States of America and abroad. They express, through their music, the pain that poor African Americans feel and what happens when one is desperately trying to eat and pay bills with a salary that is based on the minimum wage. They understand clearly how White America still enslaves African Americans and poor people. They have developed very skillful marketing practices that entice one to buy products that they cannot afford. Always the money from the poor goes back to those who are in control. They often take African Americans from the community and pay them a large salary to use whatever sounds and movements that are popular in the African American community to develop their marketing strategies. For instance, as much as they dislike the Hip Hop style, most products marketed toward youth uses Hip Hop cultural style. While upper and middle class Americans are demanding that their children change their language and dress styles, the media use Hip Hop language and dress in most of their advertisements. These slick marketing strategies cause poor people to buy too many goods on credit. Those persons with the most money get the best percentage rate on loans. Poor people get the worse interest rates. Consequently, many African Americans, poor and middle classes, pay more than fifty percent of their monthly earnings in interest payments. In other words, African Americans give back to White America, for the most part, fifty percent of their yearly earnings. They do no work for it, they just sit and wait. The artists dead prez, Lauryn Hill and Nas each speak to how our minds are controlled by the American system and the need to reclaim our African soul.

It is only through a thorough understanding of one's true history and culture can one comprehend the importance of both the Capoeira and Hip Hop movements. While each has its violent side, each has a spiritual side as well. Each emerged out of the cultural memory of their African heritage. This African heritage goes all the way back to the Kemetic ancestors who studied how everything in the universe worked. Their intent seemed to have been to always be in rhythm with the creative forces.

It is ironic that just as Stuckey (1987) described how African slaves in the United States started songs, rhythms, and dance the moment that they got off the boat, and created what he called the "Ring Shouts," where they danced in a circle to illustrate their cultural connection to the realization of the oneness of the past, present and future, the African slaves in Brazil from different countries created Capoeira that was danced in a circle.

It was the rhythm of the continuous circle that the ancient Africans understood. They studied the universe for thousands of years to discern that the human body worked the same as the celestial bodies. They realized that there were universal rhythms that governed all of creation, and that guiding each rhythm was the consciousness of the one creator. This one consciousness endowed human beings with the power to know and understand the recreative nature of the universe. Always, everything that exists is being recreated to include every cell in the human body and every star in the universe to include the sun. Our ancestors observed the circular dancing motion of the sun and moon and listened to the resulting vibrational tones and saw the colors that resulted from these vibrations. To dance in the circle with all the vibratory tones and colors was their primary goal.

To accomplish this goal, the ancient Africans symbolically developed neters that represented attributes of nature. Amon was the neter that presented the all powerful hidden one, and Ra and Ma'at were a reflection of Amon. All symbolic neters were always in pairs. It is this concept of duality that governs all human and celestial functions. According to Lugricz (1978) all creation begins with the one creative energy force. This one energy force is both male and female, positive and negative, and expands and creates specific patterns of formation. Each of the created patterns, whether it is a beautiful butterfly, or a beautiful bird, has its own rhythmic design. The Africans always heard the one-two beat, but could also hear the many other possibilities of rhythmic beats of creation. They heard the rhythmic beats of their own bodies-the one-two beat of the heart and all the rhythms of the nervous system as impulses traveled over the neurological network to move the body in ways that were astonishing. They heard these impulses sometimes as they traveled across the various synaptical gaps at a high speed in the nerve fiber where impulses are interpreted and sent to various muscle groups; but some times they heard the slow-moving impulse. In either case the melanated cells of symbolic Ra and Ma'at were always present to insure that the Africans always struggled to stay in tune with the creative forces of the universe.

In both Hip Hop and Capoeira, Africans in the Americas struggled to hear the beat of the ancestors. The Capoeiristas used the behimbau and drum to evoke the energy of the spirits to awaken the soul. Through these media they were able to open the pineal gland in the head and experience the power of the spirit world. When the Capoeirista dance to the music of the berimbau, he became one with the sounds and was engulfed with the rhythmic power of the creative forces of the universe. The Capoeirista is then able to have his body glide through space and blend into the one time of past, present and future. His body is as fluid as the liquid. The body's water combines with the water in the atmosphere. For that time, the Capoeirista's consciousness is one with the creator making him, in his mind, for that moment invincible as he dances in the roda circle becoming a spiritual force with the knowledge of every possible rhythmic body movement. The Capoeirista jumps and kicks, and all his acrobatic movements are done in the orderly rhythms of the symbolic African Orishas, "aspects of nature." He moves with nature's circular rhythm of the sun, moon and earth. These circular rhythms move through the Capoeirista's heart, nerves, and glands. His heart expands and contracts and sends blood continuously around the body. While at the same time, the sun is continuously rotating around the earth, expanding, contracting and refueling it every millisecond in time. The Capoeirista's nervous and endocrine systems connect him with other human beings and everything that exists, and he becomes one with the consciousness of his ancestors and the creator.

In the midst of African cultural confusion, the young Africans living in the United States of America used their creative genius to hear the beat of the ancestors. The Hip Hop rhythmic beats became their life lines. They felt the spirit, danced in a circle and developed what they called "Breakdancing." The movements that they created were unbelievable. They are able to perform movements with the body that would appear to defy all known mechanical principles governing human movement.

The breakdancers can spin in air or on their heads, change the direction of momentum in air, and on any hard surface, without missing the rhythmic beat. The Hip Hop artists, like the Capoeiristas, opened their pineal gland and used their melanated cells and connected their souls to the vibratory electromagnetic spiritual waves that are described by Crosley (2000) in his book entitled The Vodou Quantum Leap. This enabled them also to send well received and coordinated impulses over their neurological systems to move and articulate rhymes that tell their story. The Hip Hop generation in their music and dance made a quantum leap out of their European controlled minds, and like the Capoeiristas, they felt the many possible universal vibrational rhythmic beats.

The primary goal for young Brazilians and African Americans should be to regain all parts of their Kemetic souls. All African people need to understand what they feel and why. Such knowledge will help them to reclaim their ancient Kemetic souls. This cognitive awareness will allow African people to be in continuous rhythmic harmony and balance with the one creative conscience. If this occurs, African people will be able to develop thoughts, musical sounds, and body movements, and engage in everyday behavior patterns that are in tune with the eternal creative cosmic circle of life.

Harmony is characterized by an unmistakable sense of 'equilibrium'. Equilibrium is a state in which positive and negative forces are balanced. Ma'at is usually depicted next to a balanced scale.

The world as we know it is held together by a law that is based on the balanced dual nature of all things (wholes, units). Balance occurs between complementary opposites.

Taken from Egyptian Rhythm by Moustafa Gadalla

The Drum Beat That
Produced Beautiful Paintings
(2006)

I was invited to speak at a fundraiser for an organization by the name of Umbutu that was formed to raise money for projects in Africa. While there, I had no idea that I would be so affected by this experience.

Upon entering the building where the event was being held, I immediately heard the Divine Drummers from KRST Universal Temple. My instant focus was on a male drummer and female drummer in the group. I felt that the male drummer's tones were like those of the ancient god Tehuti and the female's tones were like those of the ancient goddess Ma'at. I heard another sister sing and play the guitar who was just awesome. The whole event reached its spiritual peak when the Anada African Drumming and Dance Group gave their performance. The drumming and dancing were just mystifying to the audience. The rhythmic drum beats produced vibrations in the room that raised all the persons present to a conscious level that we could feel the drum beat that combined joy, sadness, and the physical presence of a higher power. The drumbeats also led one to envision many colors and picture configurations. At the end of this event a very good friend, who is an artist and a drummer, took me outside of the room into the hallway. In the hallway, there were African pictures hanging on the wall, painted by a well-known artist who happens to be a very good friend.

He began to explain to me how one particular picture depicted the drumming that had just occurred. I listened carefully and was spellbound at his analysis of the African painting. He described in detail how the picture illustrated specific rhythms and that one could feel the same rhythmic vibrations in the drumbeats. I began to think about the various vibrations that determine the different colors. It became clear that a picture is created in the same fashion that all things are created. The beats of the drum provide the vibrational energy that has both a positive and negative charge. These rhythmical charges are polarized in a specific pattern to fashion energy in a specific design.

It was ironic that I had just received a painting, as an award for service to an organization, from the same artist whose picture was on the hallway wall. The painting that I was given was entitled "Feel the Spirit." The morning after the event, I looked at the painting and felt its spirit like never before. The vibrations that were creating the color images in my head were exciting. The image of a smaller mother and child on the right side of the painting spoke to me as the right brain of Ma'at, the goddess of truth, justice, balance, harmony, and reciprocity, and on the left side of the picture were male images of a father and son that spoke to me as Tehuti, the god of great knowledge. In the middle was a larger female image holding out her hand with a circular motion on the left and a feather or grasslike material in her hand reaching out on the right, with a Blues or Jazz man blowing a horn on the left. My feeling at the moment was, looking at the various combination of colors used in the painting and the organization of the figures, that I was observing spirit being blown through jazz and blues to energize the great mother in her effort to liberate our future children. Her outstretched hands illustrated the duality that initiates the polarized cosmic energy to provide the continuous re-creation of all that exist in the circle of everlasting love.

Reflections
(2006)

I remember having a conversation with a very good friend about Carol Barnes' book entitled Jazzy Melanin. The book was a novel about the drama of melanin technology. The book, in my opinion, was both entertaining and informative. My friend felt that any discourse about melanin was too serious to discuss in novel form. But I began to think about how much I enjoyed the book. In the book he told stories about the power of melanin. Sometimes I felt that he used the knowledge that he had received from his European education about melanin together with the intuitive insights that he actually gathered from the activity of his own pineal gland and melanin. Said another way, he seemed, in developing his story about melanin, to have communed with the cosmic conscience of the creator.

He told stories about how melanin inspired jazz musicians to create rhythms that were beyond amazing. He cited the fact that this music was rejuvenating for the listeners. They were empowered with new life energy that made them feel happy and glad to be alive. He further told how the rhythmic vibrations fused the individual body cells with the universal cosmic energy and for those moments the individual actually danced with the creator in perfect harmony.

I have never met Carol Barnes, but I feel very close to him. Many times in trying to write about melanin and the greatness of African people, I have found it impossible to rely solely on European logic. I don't know if there are words that one could use to thoroughly help others understand how our African ancestors interpreted the rhythmic source of universal consciousness. Perhaps intuitive stories are the only way to encourage others to feel and know the impact of music, dance, and art on the development of human conscience.

The intent of this work was to increase my knowledge of the greatness of African people by observing how we made music, danced, performed in athletics, and painted pictures. Some of the information may be more stories than truth. However, my desire was to move to a higher conscience level so that I would be able to listen to my African ancestors, particularly my mother and my father. As a result, at certain points in each of the essays I wrote what I felt at the moment. I entrusted my soul to what I would like to believe was the one universal conscience. The readers will have to discern whether they feel I was able to accomplish such an ambitious task. But whether I did or not, I would encourage all African people who have not started on the journey of determining the greatness of African people to do so. For me, thus far, this has been a divine experience.

I hope that these essays have helped the reader to understand the connection of body rhythms to the cosmic universal rhythms and to recognize that everything that exists has a rhythmic pattern. This is true whether it is a living organism or a nonliving substance, a song or dance. Each also has its own pre-designed patterns of rhythms. The old Africans surely understood this and were able to commune with the one creative conscience to hear and see many possible creative rhythmic patterns. This permitted them to create enchanting and sensational songs and dances, and to paint mesmerizing pictures.

It would be impossible for African Americans to return solely to our ancient ancestors' way of life in that we live in a much different time. However, within the context of the American system of competition and greed, we must redefine our moral and ethical principles based upon our ancestors and take control of our emotional selves to bring harmony and balance into our lives. We must hear and move to the rhythms of our own hearts and try again to connect with the one conscience of which we are all a part.

Each individual is part of the continuous creative energy of the cosmic universe. As such, we all have the potential to know all. The creator endowed us with free will to think and make choices. Unfortunately, we too often make the wrong choices that are based on acquiring money, power, and status. It is obvious that we need money to survive, but how much do we need? The greed factor is the engine that drives the economic system in America and our behavior as well. It is imperative that we strive to find balance and control over our feelings of greed and fear. Perhaps we should practice through meditation, listening to our hearts, and have a quantum conscience experience with the creative forces of the cosmic universe. This type of experience might enable us to continually achieve the same harmony and balance in our everyday lives that we temporarily experience in the astonishing and inspiring songs, dances, athletic movements, and amazing colorful and fascinating pictures that we created to survive the European act of cruel slavery.

Finally, I hope that these essays help us, as Asa Hilliard so eloquently put it, "reawaken our African minds." We have a job to do. The good part about it is that we have the blessing of the Creator, so long as we stay in harmony and balance with the principles of Ma'at.

THE CHARGE

Prologue
Afterwards Osiris came to Horus, it is said, from the under-world, and equipped and trained him for battle. Then he questioned him as to what he considered to be the finest action, and Horus said, "To succor (aid) one's father and mother when they suffered wrong."

Black Children
first children of the virgin mother
we celebrate you
we celebrate your birth
we celebrate your divinity
we bring you gifts of frankincense and myrrh
we bring you golden sandals,
not reboks
not nikes
but Golden Sandals

like the ones made for rulers
like the ones made eons ago for the boy King Tutankhamen
and Hatshpsut
when she was just a girl child
besides...
hoop dreams are not worthy of you
they have no power
hoop dreams are not dreams at all
they are what's left
when dreams are gone
they are the shell without the yolk
they are the flesh without the soul
for no man or woman that is free to chase stars

is satisfied with chasing a ball
no man or woman
that has ruled him/herself
is satisfied with being ruled by others
Black children
first children of the virgin mother
the world that witnesses your mother
is no longer the idyllic garden
of the first generation
your eyes must focus quickly
there is little time to crawl
your hands must be put
to work of men and women
not to the games of children
your mind to the challenge
rising on the horizon of human consciousness–
the europeanization of human thought
your charge is to stop the spead
of european consciousness,
europe's control over the minds
of Afrikan people

We are prisoners of European consciousness
trapped behind enemy lines
barbed wired
inside european paradigms
barbed wired
inside european space and time

look up to the heavens
and what names for the stars and planets come to mind?
Mars, Jupiter, Saturn, Pluto, Mercury, Uranus, Neptune, Venus

all european gods–
virtual monuments in the sky
reminding us of european "greatness"
now
cast your eyes downward
and behold the plants and animals of the earth
they all bear europe's latin and greek imprints
Black children
we must not be the people who walked
but left no footprints
who talked
 but had nothing meaningful to say
who labored but built nothing for themselves
and so
we lay at your feet
the builder spade and shovel
the mason's trowel and square

Africa's books of wisdom

GO NOW AND BUILD FOR ETERNITY

~ Dr. Listervelt Middleton

This was the last poem that Dr. Listervelt Middleton wrote in 1995 before his death.

Selected References

Adams, H. (1994). Ma'at returning to virture - returning to self. A Study Monograph.

Akbar, Na'im. (1994). Light from ancient Africa. Tallahassee: Mind Productions and Associates, Inc.

Asante, M.K. & Asante K.W. (1985). African culture: the rhythms of unity. London: Greenwood Press.

Almeida, B. (1986). Capoeira - A brazilian art Form (history, philosophy, and practice). Berkeley: North Atlantic Books

Barnes, C. (1993). Jazzy melanin. Houston: Melanin Technologies.

Barnes, C. (1988). Melanin: The chemical key to black greatness. Hampton Va.: UB & US Books and Things.

Bradeley, M. (1992). Chosen people from the caucasus. Chicago: Third World Press.

Chandler, W. B. (1999). Ancient future: The teachings and prophetic wisdom of the seven hermetic laws of ancient Egypt. Baltimore, MD: Black Classic Press.

Clarke, J. H. (1991). African World Revolution - Africans at the Crossroads. Trenton, N.J.: African World Press.

Chvaicer, M.T. (2002, August). The criminalization of capoeira in the nineteenth-century Brazil. The Hispanic American Historical Review, 82,(3)

Cooper, M.F., Macanic, D. & McNeil, J. (1997). Seeing jazz. San Francisco: Chronicle Books.

Crosley, R. (2000). The Vodou Quantum Leap - Alternate Realities, Power and Mysticism. St. Paul: Llewellyn Publications.

Cross, W.E. (1972). Stages in the development of black awareness: an exploratory investigation. In R. Jones (Eds.),

Black Psychology. New York: Harper & Row, Publishers.

dead prez. (2004). Lets get free, [CD]. New York: Sony Music Entertainment.

Diallo, Y. & Hall, M. (1989). The healing drum: African wisdom teachings. Rochester: Destiny Books.

Diop, C.A. (1974). The African origin of civization - myth or reality. Westport: Lawrence Hill.

Dyson, M. E. (1996). Between God and Gangsta Rap. New York: Oxford University Press.

Finch, C. S. (1998). The star of deep beginnings: The genesis of African science and technology. Decatur: Khenti.

Good, K, R.(1999). "Ill Na Nas, Goddesses and Drama Mamas", The Vibe History of Hip Hop. New York: Three Rivers Press.

Hall, M. P. (1988). The secret teachings of all ages. Los Angeles: The Philosophical Research Society.

Hinds, S.S. (1998). The history of Hip-Hop: What goes around comes around, The Source: The Magazine of Hip-Hop Music, Culture and Politics.

Hill, Lauryn, (2002). Un plugged. [CD]. New York: Sony Music Inc. Columbia Records.

Hilliard, A. G. (1995). The maroon within us - selected essays on African American community socialization. Baltimore: Black Classic Press.

Light. A. (1998). Tupac Amaru Shakur 1971 - 1996. New York: Three Rivers.

James G. M. (1988). Stolen legacy. San Francisco: Julian Richardson Associates.

Jones, Nasir, (2002). [CD]. God's son, Sony Music Inc. Columbia Records.

Kerenga, M. & Carruthers, J.H. (1986) Kemet and African

worldview. Los Angeles: University of Sankore Press.

King, M.L. (1968). Where do we go from here: chaos or community? Boston: Beacon Press.

King, R. D. (1990). African origin of biological psychiatry. Germantown: Seymour Smith.

Kroin, A. (200). Savion Glover and the transformation of tap "and da beat goes on". Valley Advocate Home Page, New Mass Media.

Lewis, J. L. (1992). Ring of liberation-deceptive discourse in brazilian capoeira. Chicago: The University of Chicago Press.

Loewen, J. W. (1996). Lies my teacher told me - Everything your American textbook got wrong. New York: Touch-stone Books.

Lubicz, R.A. (1978). Symbol and the symbolic - Ancient Egypt, and the evolution of consciousness. Rochester: Inner Tradition International.

Lubicz, R. A. (1986). A study of numbers - A guide to the creation of the universe. Rochester: Inner Traditions International.

Malone, J. (1996). Steppin' On the blues - visible African American dance. Chicago: University of Illinois Press.

Odum, H. W. & Johnson, G. B. (1969) Negro workaday song. New York: Negro University Press.

Pepper, W. F. (1995). Order to kill - The truth behind the murder of Martin Luther King Jr. New York: Warner Books.

Radin, D. (1997). The conscious universe: The scientific truth of psychic phenomena. San Francisco: Harper Collins.

Richards, D. M. (1980). Let the circle be unbroken. Trenton: The Red Sea Press.

Shabazz, J. (1992). The United States Vs. Hip-Hop, Hampton, Va.: United Bothers.

Sidran, B. (1971). Black folk. New York: Holt, Rhinehart and Winston.

Spencer, J. M. (1990). Protest and praise: sacred music of black religion. Minneapolis: Fortress Press.

Spencer, J. M. (1995). The rhythms of black fork - race, religion and pan-africanism. Trenton: African World Press.

Stuckey, S. (1987). Slave culture: nationalist theory and the foundations of black America. New York: Oxford University Press.

Warren, L. (1972). The dance of Africa. New York: Prentice Hall.

Washington, J. M. (1986). A testament of hope: The essential writings and speeches of Martin Luther King, Jr. San Francisco: Harper Collins.

White, A. (1997). Rebel for the Hell of it: The Life of Tupac Shakur. New York: Thunder's Mouth Press.

Wilson, E. (1998). "Duel of the iron mics" The Source: The Magazine of Hip-Hop Music, Culture and Politics.

Wolf, F.A. (1996). The spiritual universe: How quantum physics proves the existence of the soul. New York: Simon and Schuster.

www.ingramcontent.com/pod-product-compliance
Lightning Source LLC
Chambersburg PA
CBHW030026290326
41934CB00005B/509